CHRONICLES FROM KASHMIR

Chronicles from Kashmir

An Annotated, Multimedia Script

Nandita Dinesh

OpenBook
Publishers

https://www.openbookpublishers.com

Applied Theatre Praxis Series, Vol. 2
ISSN (Print): 2515-0758
ISSN (Online): 2515-0766

ISBN Paperback: 978-1-80064-017-7
ISBN Hardback: 978-1-80064-018-4
ISBN Digital (PDF): 978-1-80064-019-1
ISBN Digital ebook (epub): 978-1-80064-020-7
ISBN Digital ebook (mobi): 978-1-80064-021-4
ISBN XML: 978-1-80064-022-1
DOI: 10.11647/OBP.0223

Cover image: Photo by Vladimir Palyanov on Unsplash from https://unsplash.com/photos/Q8qTersW9Fk
Cover design: Anna Gatti.

Contents

Videos: Chronicles from Kashmir

1. The Condensed, Two-Hour, Film: http://hdl.handle.net/20.500.12434/7f37b8b1

2. The Beginning: http://hdl.handle.net/20.500.12434/26fe800f

3. The Experiment: http://hdl.handle.net/20.500.12434/cbac2e87

4. The Departure: http://hdl.handle.net/20.500.12434/ab436b9e

5. The Man & the Woman: http://hdl.handle.net/20.500.12434/324ada06

6. The Artists: http://hdl.handle.net/20.500.12434/f5dde0b9

7. The Incarcerated: http://hdl.handle.net/20.500.12434/69cf0a75

8. The Soldiers: http://hdl.handle.net/20.500.12434/8afdb7fe

9. The Argumentation Cultures: http://hdl.handle.net/20.500.12434/97a54d49

10. The Apples: http://hdl.handle.net/20.500.12434/619424ff

11. The Village City Love Affair: http://hdl.handle.net/20.500.12434/3afc6f47

12. The Wedding: http://hdl.handle.net/20.500.12434/fe68a6bd

13. The Curfewed Nights:
    a. Part 1: http://hdl.handle.net/20.500.12434/e9252776
    b. Part 2: http://hdl.handle.net/20.500.12434/49c94c02

14. The Pelters: http://hdl.handle.net/20.500.12434/20d5d863

15. The Banalities: http://hdl.handle.net/20.500.12434/3d6ef2d4

16. The Game Show: http://hdl.handle.net/20.500.12434/589ed14c

17. The Hideout: http://hdl.handle.net/20.500.12434/78d379e1

18. The Return: http://hdl.handle.net/20.500.12434/092182ab

19. The Disappeared & the Police: http://hdl.handle.net/20.500.12434/55ba313b

20. The Hope: http://hdl.handle.net/20.500.12434/55ba313c

GLOSSARY

Aam: Mango

Aam aadmi and aurat: Common man and woman

Anaar: Grapes

Arre: Hey

Asalaam alaikum: May peace be upon you

Beta: Son (colloquially used as the equivalent of "my dear")

Bhand Pather: Traditional folk theatre of Kashmir

Billi: Cat

Chalo: Let's go (literally) *or* Alright (colloquially)

Chooha: Mouse

Dastarkhaans: Long cloth that is set on the floor/table in order to serve food

Dil toh chahta hai: The heart wants it

Dupatta: A type of scarf

Halaat: The condition/the situation

Hartal: A strike

Hijab: Scarf worn by Muslim women

Ikhwan: Armed militia that are sponsored by the Indian government

Insh'Allah: If it is the will of God/ God willing

Jahaaz: Ship

Janab: Your Excellency (a colloquialism that is used to connote respect, regardless of the gender of the person being addressed)

Kaun Banega Crorepati: Who wants to be a millionaire?

Kehewa: A tea preparation that is particular to Kashmir

Kharghosh: Rabbit

Kurta: A tunic

Mehandi: Henna

Mohalla: Neighborhood

Namaskar: Greetings

Nimaaz: The ritualistic prayer that is performed by Muslims five times a day

Pangas: Colloquial term to refer to picking fights

Patang: Kite

Pheran: A type of tunic that is particular to Kashmir

Raat: Night

Rabab: A stringed instrument that is used in various Asian contexts

Rouf: A folk-dance form performed by women in Kashmir

Rotis: A kind of bread

Saab: Sir

Samar: Fruit

Tamatar: Tomato

Titili: Butterfly

Topi: A hat that functions as a marker of one's identity

Walaikum asalaam: And may peace be upon you as well

Wanvun: A style of choral singing that is particular to Kashmir

Wazwaan: A multi-course meal that is particular to Kashmir, served during celebratory occasions

Yakhni: A yogurt-based dish that is particular to Kashmiri cuisine

Zaalim: Oppressor

Introduction:
Chronicles from Kashmir

B. B. Yasir

Exploring the legitimate scope and space for theatre in a conflict zone like Kashmir is an extremely uphill task. It involves many social, cultural, religious, political and economic challenges, and above all, the risk to one's life, property and reputation.

Jammu and Kashmir have been a bone of contention since 1947, when this Subcontinent was divided after the termination of British rule into two new nations — India and Pakistan. This partition also forcibly divided the multi-regional but then politically united fabric of Jammu and Kashmir State, which fractured the State geographically, intellectually, socially, culturally and politically.

After the uprising of the militancy in 1988, Kashmir has become an uncontrolled conflict zone that presents multi-dimensional socio-political and humanitarian challenges, including risk to life, prosecutions and persecutions, unabated violence, military operations, and above all, uncertainty and loss of peace in the region. While peace of mind and a peaceful atmosphere is the basis for every theatrical activity, turbulent situations like these can provide rich dramatic content.

As an "insider," I would not like to say much about the history of this region, as my comments are likely to be treated as stemming from a biased viewpoint. Besides, Nandita (the "outsider") has already thrown sufficient light on the subject in her introduction, with the big question: "what is happening in Kashmir?"

Being a theatre professional and a Kashmiri nationalist, I have long felt it to be my moral obligation to give new impetus to the theatre movement of Kashmir and to carve a legitimate space for theatre after a dark era during 1990–2005. Thus my decision to establish the Ensemble Kashmir Theatre Akademi — EKTA (School of Drama & Repertory) in 2006, as a step forward in that direction. EKTA soon went on to become recognized as a national institution; the first of its kind in Kashmir.

In 2012, Nandita Dinesh — who had gone through a tough experience during her first visit to Kashmir in 2011, which had made her desperately sick and reluctant to return at first — came to see me at EKTA in Srinagar, referred to me by one of my students, who happened to be a college professor. After hearing about her work and

   https://doi.org/10.11647/OBP.0223.37

her wish to collaborate with EKTA as part of her doctoral project, we embarked on a multi-year collaboration.

It is important to remark here that providing a platform for an outsider is extremely challenging in Kashmir due to potential security risks and suspicions of secret agendas. But given my commitment to the theatre, I decided to take on these risks and to provide space open for Nandita to work with the artistes of EKTA, without putting any restrictions or limitations on the work. The only suggestion I made was that we had to be very careful about the sensitivities and sensibilities of people in Kashmir when dealing with their unimaginable suffering, while approaching the subject with honesty and constructing/deconstructing the content of the play. Such conversations formed the basis of the characters Guide #1 and Guide #2 in the play, representing the insider and the outsider views that were present at every step of the creation of "Chronicles of Kashmir".

While Nandita explains the process in detail in this book, I would like to draw your attention to some important points:

1. Being "insiders" who have lived the conflict, our Kashmiri actors and audience could easily connect with the content of the play and its immersion in everyday life in Kashmir.

2. When performing in Kashmir, every scene — however much we tried to be indirect — was immediately connected to someone's real-life experience.

3. During the process of revealing some concealed realities of Kashmir, about which I happened to be a first-hand source, the actors and the audience often reacted furiously towards Nandita and me, and suspected that we had some secret agenda.

4. There were big questions raised, even among my friendship circles within the theatre fraternity, concerning my collaboration with an (Indian) outsider who could not be deemed as "trustworthy". On many occasions, even my actors and members of EKTA asked: why are we doing such a project?

5. In spite of having been a leading pro-freedom activist, in many political and public circles I was viewed suspiciously for my approach to theatre activities that were unconventional.

6. It was also a big challenge to maintain consistency of performance in this multi-year project. Every stage included a gap of one year, and there were always new additions of content, concepts, thoughts, audiences and artists — but we did not let the spine of the play break.

From 2012 to 2014, the play was performed at the EKTA campus and all of the scenes were set in different rooms and spaces. Most of the scenes were very intense, but the movement of the audience from one space to another allowed them a sigh of relief to prepare for the next powerful scene. I don't mean that the audience was alienated from the play, as Brecht has put it, but that moving from one space to another provided them with time to connect with the action intellectually.

However, the final live performance of the play at a theatre space in Kamshet, Maharashtra, was a bitter experience in comparison with the performances in Kashmir. I do not understand why a group of high-profile police officers raided the campus, and although they did not actively disturb our performance, their arrival disturbed the audience mentally and added to the intensity of the play. It showed us all how the word "Kashmir" is disturbing for Indian authoritarian rulers.

I am sure this play will be a new milestone in the landscape of world theatre in general, and a landmark in the evolution of the contemporary theatre of Kashmir, in particular. I feel proud to be part of it, as co-author and a lead actor.

Bhawani Bashir Yasir
Srinagar-Kashmir (J&K)
Pin-190005, India.

Summaries and Deconstructions

What is happening in Kashmir?

A deceptive simple query to which there are no simple answers.

Like other complex issues that leave their considerers perplexed for stretches of time, the answer to the question "What is happening in Kashmir?" depends on a range of factors. It depends on who is being asked the question. It depends on who is doing the asking. It depends on the context in which the question is being asked — the place, the time, the perceived intentionality, and the audience.

Answering a question about what is happening in Kashmir is complicated because there are myriad ways in which the region's story has been told and re-told. To choose only one of these versions would give the reader an incomplete picture; it would create a false sense of certainty about a conundrum that has perplexed the finest of minds, for decades.

So, in an attempt to highlight the polyvocality that has been so crucial both to *Chronicles from Kashmir's* development and to my own understanding of the region, there follows a less-than-conventional approach to framing Kashmir's historical and contemporary socio-political condition. In this less-than-conventional approach, a one-paragraph summary of the conflict is deconstructed, in order to performatively communicate the various layers of what has happened/ is happening/ is understood as happening in the region of Kashmir.

Before going into the summary and its deconstructions, I have to tell the reader that my knowledge of these different layers of Kashmir's condition stems primarily from formal interviews and informal conversations with a range of individuals within and outside Kashmir, with a healthy sprinkling of archival research. My process of understanding Kashmir's history has been theatre-based, subjective, and fragmented, and it is precisely this lens that I would like to share with the reader of this book. So, embrace the subjectivity that follows. It is intentional; it is problematic; it is, to me, more real than any declarations of certainty and fact when it comes to understanding Kashmir.[1]

---

1   Readers who would like a more scholarly starting point to explore Kashmir's histories are encouraged to consider the range of reading material that has been included in the Installations and referenced in the Bibliography. It is not in line with the ethos of this work to make a prescriptive suggestion about where one should begin — so use your discretion; pick your starting point!

                    https://doi.org/10.11647/OBP.0223.01

Since one version of events is not an option, let's start with a very general summary — a summary that can then be pulled apart.

1. Perhaps the most well-known version of Kashmir's history is the one in which recent conflicts are described as being rooted in the Partition of 1947, when the Hindu ruler of a majority Muslim region initially refused to join either of the newly created nation-states of India or Pakistan.

2. This initial refusal changed when Pakistani forces invaded Kashmir a few years later, causing the Hindu ruler to approach India for assistance — assistance that was offered on the condition that Kashmir would accede to the Indian nation-state.

3. The Indian Prime Minister, Jawaharlal Nehru, is said to have assured Kashmiris that this accession would be temporary and last only until law and order returned to the region.

4. This assurance also included a promise that, when law and order returned to the region, a plebiscite would be held so that the people of Kashmir could decide their fate.

5. Would they want to join India? Pakistan? Or function as an independent nation-state?

That's the reductive, less complex version. But now, let's break those ideas apart, shall we?

---

1. Perhaps the most well-known version of Kashmir's history is the one in which the conflicts are described as being rooted in the Partition of 1947, when the Hindu ruler of a majority Muslim region initially refused to join either of the newly created nation-states of India and Pakistan.

   - There are others who say that the region of Kashmir — comprised of Jammu, the parts of the Kashmir Valley that are currently within Indian borders, Ladakh, the parts of the Kashmir Valley that are currently within Pakistani borders, Gilgit, and Baltistan — has never been conflict-free. According to this view, there have always been conflicts between the different groups inhabiting Kashmir, and many of today's tensions existed much before Partition. It is the historical conflicts, these opinion-holders suggest, that underpin the ongoing stalemate that exists when it comes to solving the region's problems.

   - There are others who say that the region was, historically, a centre of religious syncretism and that it is the communal agendas of India and Pakistan that have caused a seemingly unresolvable situation in which positions are being drawn based on religious lines. In this view, the religion of the ruler during Partition was politicized in relation to the religious composition of his citizens — a politicization that has since rendered a chasm across the region and the subcontinent. Part of the argument that is contained within this narrative is that Kashmiris have historically been unique; different; embodying a *Kashmiriyat* (Kashmiri-ness, for the lack of a better translation) that has been threatened by forces of communalism. So, for those who agree with this view, all the regions of Jammu and Kashmir belong together, as an autonomous nation-state. Kashmiris are not, and have never been, Indian or Pakistani.

- There are those who say that the region of Kashmir should have gone to Pakistan as soon as Partition occurred. And that it was the placement of power in the hands of minority groups that did not allow this natural affiliation to take place.

- Then, there are the arguments that fall somewhere between all of the above.

---

2. This initial refusal changed when Pakistani forces invaded Kashmir a few years later, causing the Hindu ruler to approach India for assistance — assistance that was offered on the condition that Kashmir would accede to the Indian nation-state.

- Could the event be called an invasion if scores of people in the region wanted to join Pakistan to begin with, but were disallowed because of their Hindu ruler?

- And if it wasn't an invasion, what was it?

- How might we interpret India's involvement at the behest of a monarch, rather than his citizens?

- Did the Hindu ruler truly come to India for temporary assistance? Or did he, knowing that his citizens would otherwise never agree to an accession to India, use Pakistani aggression as an excuse for accession?

- What are the ethics of the Indian Prime Minister's offer, in asking for an agreement of such massive gravity, at a time when Kashmir's ruler had his back against a wall?

- Then, there are the questions that are offshoots and derivatives of all of the above.

3. Indian Prime Minister, Jawaharlal Nehru, is said to have assured Kashmiris that this accession would be temporary and last only until law and order returned to the region.

   • Some speak to a continued involvement by the Indian government in perpetuating Kashmir's turmoil precisely to prevent the return of law and order. After all, if law and order never return to Kashmir, the pre-conditions for the plebiscite will never be met.

   • The counterargument that is offered here, of course, is that law and order are never achievable because of Pakistan's involvement in the region (not India's).

   • Who would decide that law and order have come to prevail in Kashmir? Would that status need to be decided and verified by the UN? Or would it be a status that needs to be declared and agreed upon by the governments of India and Pakistan (and China, for the parts of Ladakh that fall within its control)?

   • Then, there are the questions that are offshoots and derivatives of all of the above.

---

4. An assurance that also included a promise that, when law and order returned to the region, a plebiscite would be held so that the people of Kashmir could decide their fate.

   • Even in the unlikely event that a plebiscite is under consideration, which Kashmiris are we talking about? The Kashmiris who live in the Valley that is under Indian administration? Does that also include the citizens of Hindu-dominated Jammu and Buddhist-majority Ladakh? Does the pool of plebiscite respondents also include the Kashmiris who live in Pakistan-administered Kashmir, Gilgit, and Baltistan? What about the Kashmiris who live in the part of Ladakh that is contested by China? What about the huge Kashmiri Diaspora that now inhabits regions across the world, many of whom — the Kashmiri Pandits (Hindus) in particular — are said to have been driven out of the Valley in fear for their lives? When we talk about carrying out a plebiscite, which Kashmiris are we referring to?

   • Who would conduct the plebiscite? How would it be implemented? Who would monitor the results? What would be the plan for transition, for each of the possible outcomes?

   • Then, there are the questions that are offshoots and derivatives of all of the above.

5. Would they want to join India? Pakistan? Or function as an independent nation-state?

- What options are on the ballot for the plebiscite (should it ever happen)?

- Some say that Kashmiris only get to choose between India and Pakistan. Others insist that there is, and always has been, a third option: an autonomous Kashmiri nation-state.

- And if all these conundrums weren't enough, in August 2019, the Indian government revoked an Act that gave the region of Jammu & Kashmir special status in the Indian constitution — an Act that ensured that the complexities surrounding the resolution of Kashmir's conflicts were acknowledged, albeit symbolically. With this Act's revocation, Kashmir's fate has become even more unpredictable. If Kashmir has now been absorbed into the Indian nation-state, unilaterally, is the government even bound to acknowledge that a conflict exists?

If one summary can be deconstructed in so many ways, imagine how many more summaries could be written and rewritten, deconstructed and reconstructed.

So, what is happening in Kashmir? Many, many things.

And just like the conflicts that drove its creation, there is no simplified way to speak about the evolution of *Chronicles from Kashmir*.

The summary is this. Between 2011 and 2018, *Chronicles from Kashmir* evolved:

- from being a doctoral project to becoming a longer-term undertaking;

- from being a piece with no particular durational restrictions, to becoming a 24-hour immersive experience;

- from being a play conceptualized for the theatre, to straddling the worlds of theatre, writing, film, and education.

This summary, just like the one that came before, needs to be deconstructed. This time around though, it might be easier to take the summary apart through a linear timeline.

Before doing so, I should inform the reader that I have written extensively about my work in Kashmir. And like most acts of re-telling, there are slight differences each time that I (re)tell the story. Sometimes, moments that were once considered to be essential, fade in their importance. Sometimes, occurrences that were once glossed over, seem more deserving of attention. Each time I talk about *Chronicles from Kashmir* — a project that has consumed my life for almost a decade — the narrative is the same, but different.

2009

Sometime in 2009, a friend sent me a copy of Griselda Gambaro's (1992) *Information for Foreigners* (IFF); the same friend who also sent me Susan Haedicke's (2002) article about the immersive work, *Un Voyage Pas Comme Les Autres Sur Le Chemins De'l Exil* (*Chemins*). This friend clearly knew my aesthetic preferences before I could even articulate them myself.

Reading Gambaro and Haedicke struck a chord, and from the time that I encountered *IFF* and *Chemins*, I have been consumed by:

- immersive aesthetics — works that are multisensorial and alter traditional modes of engagement between audience and spectators;

- the use of the promenade — where the audience walks from one space to another rather than engaging with a performance in one, predetermined location and position;

- site-responsive strategies — where performances take place in response to unexpected spaces.

Beginning in 2009, in every theatre project that I undertook, I would try to find a way to include these elements — sometimes successfully; most of the time, not so successfully. It was a time in my practice when I could not articulate <u>why</u> these particular aesthetic choices spoke to me. All I knew was that they did, and that I had to explore them.

2011

My very first visit to Kashmir was by way of Jammu, where I began my time in the region by conducting theatre workshops with young girls in a home for orphans. Jammu, I thought at the time, would be a gentler first entry to the region before jumping directly into the intensities of what was happening in Kashmir. Eventually, the administrators of this organization invited me to visit a similar home that was operated by their organization in Kashmir; a home that was a few kilometres form the border with Pakistan.

And so, I landed in Kupwara in the harshness of winter, and fell terribly sick.

Most of what I remember from that trip is through a haze of watering eyes, nose, and throat. I think I was taken to a funeral. I think I got stuck in the middle of a protest on my way to the airport. I think I got questioned by an army officer about why I wanted to visit Kashmir.

I don't remember much. At all. My first visit to Kashmir was a complete blur.

2012

After that not-so-great first visit, I didn't think I would return to Kashmir. Until a colleague reached out. This colleague was visiting India from the UK and wanted to conduct a theatre workshop in Kashmir. Somehow, she convinced me that I should go with her, as a collaborator. And so, I returned.

The same organization that I had worked with the previous year agreed to host us, in a different city this time: Anantnag. And while the project got off to a very slow start, with neither of us thinking that anything more than a few theatre-games-based workshops with the young women would be possible, circumstances slowly began to shift.

Suddenly we found ourselves meeting people, running additional workshops, forming wonderful friendships, and being connected to theatre folks around the Valley — one of whom was the director of the Ensemble Kashmir Theatre Akademi (EKTA); an ensemble that would become my partner for years to come.

As these connections developed, so did my thinking about the role for theatre within the Kashmiri context. Would it be possible for Indian army soldiers to immerse themselves (theatrically) in the life of Kashmiri civilians? And if they did, would such an immersion enable them to become more empathetic in the way they carried out their jobs? Would it be possible for militants to step, theatrically, into the shoes of soldiers in the Indian army? Could Immersive Theatre, in this context, become a powerful way for Others to engage in perspectives and experiences that they had not lived themselves?

With grandiose ideas for how theatre could intervene in the region, and a newfound potential partner in EKTA, I realized that I needed to develop a critical framework to better articulate my considerations. After all, creating cross-community Immersive Theatre works in an active conflict zone needed some rigorous analysis and design. Enter the decision to pursue a doctoral project and to frame that undertaking as a theatrical exploration of the grey zones in Kashmir's conflicts.[2] The grey zones — the

---

2 For a detailed account of the specific trajectory of my explorations, and their positioning within the larger arena of Theatre & Performance studies, please see *Theatre & War* (Dinesh, 2013), available Open Access, http://www.doi.org/10.11647/OBP.0099

areas of murkiness where traditional understandings of victimhood and perpetration need to be questioned — in relation to soldiers, militants, and civilians in Kashmir.

2013

This year saw my first collaboration with EKTA and the first time that I had to systematize the process of conducting a formal workshop around Immersive Theatre. Given the newness of these challenges and partnerships, I decided to start my collaboration with EKTA by focusing on the most accessible of three identity groups that I wanted to work with: civil society.

The workshop's focus on understanding the civilian experience in Kashmir was informed by the ensemble members in the workshop, civilians who shared various aspects of their experience with me; I realized that these experiences revealed many blurred boundaries between the more obvious identity groupings of civilian, soldier, and militant. The month-long process led to the creation an immersive performance about women's experiences in the region; a performance entitled *Pinjare* (*Cages*) that could only admit two spectators at a time, and that was targeted toward male, Kashmiri spectators.

In addition to this focus on aestheticizing the grey zones of civilian experience, 2013 was also the year in which I started— always in consultation with my colleagues at EKTA— creating future theatrical partnerships with Kashmiri militants and with soldiers in the Indian Army. And while my attempts to reach active militants failed, my attempts to reach the army did not. A Brigadier agreed to speak with me, to chat about the potential for arts-based practices in the training of soldiers; he also agreed to attend a performance of *Cages*. This was all before I left Kashmir, of course. After I left, the Brigadier simply became impossible to reach.

As many project initiators do, I learned more from my failures than my successes. From my failure to reach the militants, I realized that there was no way an active militant would agree to speak with me and that even if they did, all of us would be at too much risk. From the failed conversations with the Brigadier, I eventually learned about the ways in which armies tend to isolate themselves. From intense conversations with audience members of *Cages*, I slowly began to unpack the sheer extent of the politics in which I was embroiled by my very presence in Kashmir: as a woman; as an Indian.

2014

When I returned to EKTA in 2014, the goal was to figure out how to include the voices of militants, when active militants would not or could not engage with me. I quickly realized that *former* militants were perhaps the only group that would be able/willing to meet with me; creating material for a Documentary Theatre piece about former militants thus became the focus of that year's collaboration with EKTA.

Upon connecting with an organization that works for the welfare of former militants, two EKTA actors and I travelled to parts of Kashmir I had never been to before: homes that lay inside small villages; homes that were far away from witnesses; homes in which former militants talked to me about their particular experiences. They described why they had joined the militancy; what they were fighting for; why they had decided to leave.

I did all of this not realizing that I was stepping into a veritable minefield. That listening to the voices of these men and their wives, as an Indian woman, was going to spark reactions that I did not even know to expect, let alone predict. Although the process of creating *Meri Kahani Meri Zabani* (*My Story, My Words; MKMZ*) was incredibly rewarding for myself and for the actors — and seemingly for the folks we had interviewed — things changed quickly, intensely, and in a volatile fashion.

The man who was my primary contact in facilitating interviews with the former militants disappeared after the first showing of *MKMZ*. The post-performance discussions with audience members who had not been involved in the interviews became explosive. And quickly, I realized that I had to question both my right to tell the stories that I was telling, and my dubious decision to share those narratives with people who had borne the brunt of each other's traumas for decades. Suddenly, I had to acknowledge the idea that the work I was making in Kashmir might not be for Kashmiri audiences; that my grandiose notions of sharing work about an Other with an Other, in that context, was impossible.

So I left EKTA that year, considering two potential target audiences for the work we were creating: an audience of young Kashmiris who might be more willing and able to engage with content about the histories of their land; an audience of non-Kashmiris, like myself, who did *not* have the lived experience of war and needed to learn more about the region in order to become better allies, in whatever way we could.

That's the primary question with which I left Kashmir in 2014: for whom were EKTA and I creating this work? And how could we do a more effective job of framing it for its target audiences? Did we need to consider a pre-performance workshop of some kind, to ensure that our spectators — especially in Kashmir — had the chance to hear about our intentions and objectives, before being immersed in the work?

2014 was also the year in which I accepted the fact that my overtures to reach out to the Indian Armed Forces in Kashmir were likely to go unacknowledged. So, what were the voices in the army that would engage with me? Where were the Armed Forces personnel who had the time and ability to do so, rather than being constantly on alert in an active conflict zone? Who were the sub-group of soldiers in the Indian Armed Forces that I could access, given the specific resources that I had at my disposal? With these questions in mind, there was only target group that I could work with: cadets in training at a Defence Academy in western India. So, that's what I did. A process that led to a creation called *Waiting*, composed from monologues written by the young men: for what/whom were they waiting?

The rest of 2014 was spent collating and curating the material that had emerged from the previous years' collaborations with EKTA, my work with the cadets, and experiences from my visits to Kashmir in 2011 and 2012. Slowly, a script began to form, in dialogue with a work that I had been obsessed with for a long time: Griselda Gambaro's *IFF*.[3]

As a first step, I sat with Gambaro's work and forced myself to adapt each of her scenes in a way that would make sense for Kashmir. At this stage, I very much considered the work as an adaptation of *IFF*, rather than a new work that simply used Gambaro's script as inspiration.

2015

The first iteration of our Kashmiri adaptation of *IFF* stuck closely to the source material. But as most plays tend to do, the shape of the text morphed as soon as it was in the actors' hands and voices; we collaboratively designed ideas that altered both the form and content of Gambaro's work. Suddenly, I realized that Gambaro's play was nothing more or less than a point of departure for us. Our *IFF* was a different play. And while a couple of the scenes functioned as adaptations (*The Experiment* and *The Man & the Woman*) our *IFF* had started to grow into its own aesthetic.

But once again, despite a rewarding process of exchange and collaborative development with EKTA, the response from the audience members was explosive.

The adult audiences that were composed of members of Srinagar's theatre community rejected the fragmented, promenade form: the distance from Realism troubled this audience; it is possible that their discomfort was gravely magnified by my being Indian. "You can never imagine what we have lived through," was the response that seemed underscore it all. And they were right, of course; I cannot.

---

3   Gambaro's play about the Dirty War in Argentina takes place in the promenade, is site-specific, and focuses on the politics and ethics of witnessing acts of violence.

This year, though, learning from the lessons of years past, we also made sure to work with a younger audience: high-school students in Srinagar who, we thought, were distant enough from the material to engage with it differently. And once again, we were wrong: "This is not our past," the young people said. "The things that you're showing us are still happening. They are not history. They are our present. Why are you showing us what we are already living with?"

Listening to the young people was illuminating. They were able — through their youthful articulation — to enable me to understand what the adults, with their emotional intensity, had not managed to communicate. Nothing I could create in Kashmir, if it was about Kashmir, could be for Kashmiris. It would have to be for others like myself. Non-Kashmiris. Foreigners. Outsiders.

2016

When I returned to Kashmir a year after that revelation about target audience and audience framing, the mission was to return to EKTA and to sculpt *IFF* — which had now been renamed *Information for/from Outsiders: Chronicles form Kashmir* — for an audience of outsiders.

Unfortunately, this was not to be. Two days before the workshop was set to commence, a young rebel/militant/terrorist/leader (depending on who you ask) was killed by the Indian Army. And just like that, a curfew was declared in the Valley.

I had been in Kashmir during the occasional strike or protest in years past, and these events had led us to cancel rehearsals and the occasional performance. But 2016 was different. This year, there seemed to be no end in sight to the protests. There seemed to be no way for the actors to reach the theatre's premises for the workshop. The two actors who already happened to be at the facility were so distracted and stressed that trying to create smaller-scale versions of the workshop simply didn't work. And somewhere in the middle of all of these events, when we were having wide-ranging conversations about the future of *IFF*, I asked a colleague: "What if this became a 24-hour performance?"

I did not expect his response: "Why not?"

And just like that, on a curfew night in Kashmir, the vision for a 24-hour piece came alive.

I have since been able to articulate that decision in more eloquent ways: the impact of durational immersion on spectators; the necessity of duration in communicating fragmentation and complexity; the necessity of duration in fostering experiential understanding.

But on that night, when the idea first came up, it was almost a whim. There was a curfew. There was nothing else to do. And so, we imagined.

2017

From the day after my colleague and I had that conversation, I wrote. In bits and pieces. In scenes and fragments. No longer were *IFF* or *Chemins* useful to me as points of reference. This was a new beast.

In mid-2017, with a rough draft of a script for a 24-hour performance in hand, the ensemble and I decided to meet somewhere else in the subcontinent, outside Kashmir. After all, hadn't we all realized that the play would be more suitable for an audience of non-Kashmiris?

We went to the only place that would agree to host such an effort, which was also the only place that we could afford. So, in July 2017, a team of about twelve artists went to Kamshet, in western India. The plan was simple: we would workshop the draft that I had been working on for the past year and, ideally, we would test drive an initial version of the 24-hour performance for an audience of non-Kashmiris.

We didn't know if we could make it happen. We didn't know if we'd actually manage to pull all of this off in less than a month. But, somehow, with the collective commitment of an ensemble, *Chronicles from Kashmir* came together.

At the end of an intense period of rehearsal and rewrites, we were able to share a trial performance with a group of audience members that included individuals who knew us, and who were willing to be part of the "dress rehearsal," as it were. This was the first time we had been able to try the entire 24-hour event with a live audience and the "dress rehearsal" was seminal in our understanding of an event that we had, until then, been only able to rehearse in fragments.

We made a lot of mistakes with that audience; we learned and adapted and re-rehearsed for the next performance: this time for many audience members with whom we did not have prior relationships, and some of whom had travelled for over a day, by train, to get to the experience.

We started the second performance and were only about halfway through the first scene when the police showed up.

The first two policemen who walked in were in plain clothes and I had no reason to think that they were anyone but audience members who were arriving late. But they were police, they said; officers who ushered me out of the performance space so that they could inform me in hushed tones that they had been told about a group of Kashmiris doing something that warranted attention. They had been informed, the police said, that a 'foreign' director was in-charge.

"Can we see your visa?"

"I don't need a visa. I have an Indian passport."

"Oh."

Was it the amplified sound of the *azaan* in a Hindu-dominated locality that caused someone to report us to the police? Was it the sound of fireworks, in conjunction with the sound of the Muslim call to prayer, that set off alarm bells? Or was it a simple case of bias and prejudice and factionalism?

Whatever the case, to this day, we do not know who called the police on *Chronicles from Kashmir*. All we know is that the police showed up and, suddenly, our theatrical accomplishment became something else. Something unnerving.

The police were a continued presence at the second performance of *Chronicles from Kashmir,* adding a chilling layer of reality to the content that was being explored. My phone calls to well-placed colleagues went to naught.

"This is not an India in which our connections work," I was told.

"Get out of there now. Before they file a criminal case against you, and you cannot leave the country."

A criminal case against me? For what? Hadn't I offered to let the police officers read the script? Hadn't I told them that they were welcome to stay? Weren't they the ones who refused my invitations because the script was too long to read?

"Did they take any pictures?"

"Well, yes, they took some pho —"

"You shouldn't have let them do that. You never know how they are going to use them. Can you leave now? Can you get out of the country?"

We were in hour 12 of the performance. The police had left in hour 7. Maybe the storm had passed.

They returned though, in hour 19. And this time, they wanted names. What were the names of the artists who had created this performance, and what were our addresses? What were the names of the audience members, and what were their addresses?

These were the questions that scared us.

We knew there were some risks to the work that we had undertaken, but we didn't expect to have to identify our spectators to the police. We knew that talking about Kashmir could be controversial, but we did not think that it would bring authoritarian voices to our doors. After all, one of the reasons we had decided to go outside Kashmir this year was to give the actors a break... from curfews, and strikes, and fear. But here we were. Doused in the very fear that we were trying to escape.

In a time when Indian newspapers were publishing a fairly regular dose of articles about Muslims being lynched upon suspicion of eating beef, we were terrified. It would have been one thing if the risk was only to me, or to some of the more experienced members of the ensemble who better understood the risks. But it was quite something else when the risks were for an entire company. It was quite something else when the risk was shared by a 16-year old who had partly signed up for this project simply to go outside Kashmir — he had never done that before.

When the risks begin to include so many others besides oneself — including audience members — standing up to the establishment does not seem idealistic or passionate. It just seems stupid.

So, given the fear that was permeating the cast, given that our audience the next day was going to be composed of students from a local high school, we decided to call off the next performance of *Chronicles from Kashmir*.

We have not been able to perform the work, live, since then.

2018

When multiple festivals and future host organizations in the Indian subcontinent turned down our proposals to perform in their spaces, always citing safety as the reason behind their reticence, our goal became to find new ways to keep the work alive. Through the written script. And, we decided, through film.

So, after a year of fundraising and connecting and hustling, we were ready to shoot a film version of *Chronicles from Kashmir*, a month before the script was set to be published in Mumbai.

Once again, we began our time together with great hope: the hope that this year would be different; the hope that the time away from Kashmir, shooting the film, would be rejuvenating for the ensemble.

But, once again, our hopes came to naught.

Two weeks into our shooting schedule, with one week left to go, I received a message from the educational institution that was hosting us.

"You need to leave tomorrow," I was told. "Journalists in this area are asking questions about why we have Kashmiris shooting a film here. This is a Hindu-dominated area. There have been issues in the past. We cannot take any risks."

"We cannot afford to change our tickets and leave tomorrow. I simply don't have the money to make that happen."

"Maybe we can pay for you to leave?"

"Or maybe we could find a compromise? What if we agreed to restrict our filming to the building in which we are being hosted? You know, what if we voluntarily place ourselves under house arrest of sorts, only coming close to your premises when we need to bring food back up for the ensemble?"

"Maybe that would work."

For the next week, ten of us undertook an inexplicable form of voluntary house arrest. From having access to an entire campus to shoot *Chronicles from Kashmir*, suddenly, we only had one building and the area surrounding it. We couldn't go outside that area for fear of being seen. And being asked to leave.

Between this residential situation, and a simultaneous ban that Facebook imposed on our publisher, prohibiting them from selling the about-to-be-launched first edition of the script on their online marketplace, we found ourselves — again — in the eye of a storm. A storm that had come about so subtly, so unexpectedly, that I still have trouble believing the extent of the fuss that went into censoring a small group of people who were coming together to make theatre.

None of us have names that call attention. None of us come from high-powered spheres of influence and celebrity status. We were — we are — simple folk.

What was all the fuss about?

2019–2020

The first edition of the script exists.

The film exists, in a heavily condensed two-hour-long form and as additional stand-alone segments from the 24-hour experience.

And here we are.

At another turning point in Kashmir's history — the abrogation of Article 370 — when things are more unpredictable than they've ever been.

When the government's unilateral decision to revoke Kashmir's special status in August 2019 left the region without phone lines for two months.

When, as I write this, the internet remains disconnected and schools remain closed and life remains crippled.

So, here we are.

As artists and as educators.

Wondering, now what?

"Now what?" has led to this second edition of *Chronicles from Kashmir* that includes more than the script for a performance. An edition that includes:

Links to videos of Chronicles from Kashmir	Discussion questions for the reader to better understand Kashmir and this work	Practical exercises for the reader to gain experiential insight into *Chronicles from Kashmir's* aesthetic and pedagogical strategies	Words in translation from Hindustani (a combination of Hindu and Urdu that makes both languages accessible to speakers of either)

"Now what?" has led us to decide that we want more learners, within and outside formal educational environments, to use our script as the jumping-off point to engage with a larger study of what is happening in Kashmir.

"Now what?" has brought us here. To this.

I write this introduction as my colleagues in Kashmir continue to remain under varying forms of lockdown.

I write this introduction after more than a year of wondering whether or not I have the energy to deal with the potential backlash that a second edition might provoke.

I write this introduction after I was finally able speak to my colleagues in EKTA, after months of no communication, and realize that our time together couldn't end like this. Without "more."

"More."
More hope.
More struggle.
More collaboration.
More imagination.

"More."
There has to be "more."

Right?

Nandita Dinesh

A Note on Adaptation & Design

- If you are approaching this piece as a complete outsider to the conflicts it speaks of, **PLEASE** engage with Kashmiris — and others with experience of Kashmir — in your local context. They will be best positioned to guide you on elements that you do not understand.

  If your local experts disagree with some/many aspects of this text, you are welcome to adapt/edit/change the material and to make choices that seem most ethical in your context.

  If there is no one that you are able to engage with locally, and you find yourself in need of guidance, please reach out to us: ChroniclesFromKashmir@gmail. com

- Every aspect of *Chronicles from Kashmir* has been intentionally crafted to be flexible. So, be as creative as you want in interpreting directions: costuming, props, set, lighting, song, character changes, and the use of Urdu/Hindustani terms. Use what makes sense in your context; use what you can afford; use what you have access to.

The Schedule

5:30 PM	6:00 PM	Bus picks up spectators and arrives
6:00 PM	6:40 PM	Scene 0
6:40 PM	7:00 PM	Scene 1
7:00 PM	7:20 PM	Scene 2
7:20 PM	7:40 PM	Scene 3
7:40 PM	8:10 PM	Installation A
8:10 PM	8:30 PM	Scene 4
8:30 PM	8:50 PM	Scene 5
8:50 PM	9:20 PM	Installation B
9:20 PM	9:40 PM	Scene 6
9:40 PM	10:00 PM	Scene 7
10:00 PM	10:20 PM	Scene 8
10:20 PM	11:00 PM	The First Coalition
11:00 PM	11:20 PM	Scene 9

Notice the time at which the performance begins, and the subsequent impact on how the rest of the experience unfolds.

What are the pedagogical benefits/drawbacks of the chosen timeframe? For example: would there be different impacts if Part 2 of *A Wedding and a Curfewed Night* occurred from 10 PM to 6 AM, rather than 4 AM to 12 PM?

https://doi.org/10.11647/OBP.0223.02

11:20 PM	11:40 PM	Scene 10
11:40 PM	12:00 AM	Installation C
12:00 AM	12.20 AM	The Second Coalition
12.30 AM	2 AM	Scene 11
2:00 AM	4 AM	A Wedding and a Curfewed Night: Part 1
4:00 AM	12 PM	A Wedding and a Curfewed Night: Part 2
12:10 PM	12:30 PM	Scene 12
12:30 PM	1:10 PM	The Third Coalition
1:10 PM	1:30 PM	Scene 13
1:30 PM	1:50 PM	Scene 14
1:50 PM	2:10 PM	Scene 15
2:10 PM	2:40 PM	Installation D
2:40 PM	3:00 PM	Scene 16
3:00 PM	3:20 PM	Scene 17
3:20 PM	3:50 PM	Installation E
3:50 PM	4:10 PM	Scene 18
4:10 PM	4:30 PM	Scene 19
4:30 PM	4:50 PM	Scene 20
4:50 PM	5:10 PM	Scene 21
5:10 PM	5:40 PM	Scene 22
5:40 PM	6:10 PM	The Last Coalition
6:00 PM		Bus leaves

Different contexts create different understandings of how the hours of a day should be used: which hours are for sleep, for instance, and which hours are for activity? Understanding these particularities can be important for creators to more effectively time events so as to heighten desired impacts.

If you were going to stage *Chronicles from Kashmir* in your local context, how would you adapt this schedule?

The Journey Begins

It is important that all fifteen spectators to Information for/from Outsiders: Chronicles from Kashmir *arrive at the same time. The group should be asked to meet at a predetermined spot, at 5.30 PM, with prior knowledge of the following information.*

Participants can expect:

- Walking and physical exertion.
- Interaction with the performers.
- Regular provision of food and drink.
- Time to sleep, if they choose.
- Access to washrooms.

Participants should:

- Wear comfortable shoes.
- Have some form of government-issued photo identification.
- Pack one change of clothes and a towel.
- Carry medication for any pre-existing health conditions.

- Bring extra water/snacks, if they need time-regulated food/drink.
- Make sure they have other location-specific materials (like raingear), based on weather conditions in the performance context.

> What would be the potential impacts of *not* sending this information to spectators before their arrival at the event?

https://doi.org/10.11647/OBP.0223.03

Participants should not:

- Carry phones or any other technological devices: it is recommended that they let near and dear ones know that they will be out of touch for a day. In case of emergencies, the number for one crew member can be provided.

- Bring any materials that might be used as diversions from the experience (such as books, for example): all materials will be subject to inspection and approval by a member of the production team.

Consider the notion of 'care' in relation the audience for a durational, immersive, theatrical experience.

When does the process of caring start?

How does it manifest?

When does it end?

A bus arrives to take spectators to the performance space, and as audience members line up to board the bus, an ACTOR checks their IDs against names on the guest list. The ACTOR then checks the spectators' bags to ensure that there are no unauthorized, 'diversionary' materials that are being brought in. Such material should be returned to the audience member's private vehicle and/or confiscated by the ACTOR to be kept in a lockbox on the bus until the audience departs the next day.

Rabab
A stringed instrument that is used in various Asian contexts

Once IDs and belongings are cleared, the ACTOR says to each guest as they board the bus: "Welcome." Nothing more. Nothing less.

On the bus, rabab *music plays until audience members arrive at the performance location.*

Once at the final destination, audience members are instructed to leave all their belongings on the bus. They are told that the production team will move their belongings to a location where spectators can have access to them at any time. "Just ask the GUIDES if you need access to your belongings during the experience," the ACTOR tells them.

The ACTOR then takes audience members to a space that is designed as a tourism office and is filled with predictable paraphernalia about sights that they might encounter in Kashmir.

While audience members begin their experience in the tourism office, the production team moves their belongings from the bus and stores them in a central location. If/when spectators make requests for their belongings, one of the GUIDES calls for a crew member to walk the spectator over to that storage location. It is suggested that there should be two crew members who are always *on audience duty, so that they can be the ones to facilitate/manage any unforeseen requests/incidents that might arise for specific spectators — leaving the GUIDES and other audience members to carry on with the experience.*

The narratives in *Chronicles from Kashmir* have been crafted
with a careful approach to balance.

A lot of care was taken to understand
how many of each type of narrative
(victim, perpetrator, the grey zones between/within)
to include from **each identity group**
(Indian Armed Forces, Civil Society, Militants).

The objective of the calculation was this:
How could we ethically address the reality that some people suffer more than others
(civilians, primarily), without resorting to overly simplistic categorizations of victim
and perpetrator?

For instance, how many scenes would need to highlight civilians as victims, in order
for us to be ethically able to include one scene elsewhere in the performance in
which a soldier from the Armed Forces is not depicted solely as a perpetrator?

So, as an exercise, create a table like this:

	Victim	*Perpetrator*	*Grey Zones*
Armed Forces	.		
Civil Society			
Militants			

As you read the scenes, make a tally of which perspective is being shown
in each one.

Yes, some scenes could be categorized in multiple columns.
Many of them will depend on your interpretation.
But do the counting. Just as an exercise.
And see what such an approach might reveal.

Scene 0
Framing the Experience

⊙ WATCH THE VIDEO

Throughout the 24-hour experience, the azaan *— the Muslim call to prayer — must occur at appropriate times. There should be a designated actor, or recording, giving the call to prayer. Actors who are not performing in that instance, or who are in scenes where the context allows, should pray…if they want to.*

When they disembark from the bus, audience members are taken to a space that is designed as a tour operator's office and is filled with paraphernalia that the "mainstream" tourism industry might tell outsiders to expect in Kashmir. It is important that this space, at the beginning, is "touristy" — that it extolls the natural beauty of the Valley and her peoples; that it reinforces stereotypes, if you will. This is important so as to highlight the layers that will be added to the design of this same space by the end of the 24-hour experience.

What are the complexities inherent in invoking religion/spirituality as a performance strategy?

How do these complexities shift based on the religiosity/ perceived religiosity of the context in which the work is created/ performed?

There are refreshments that are served here; music is playing (perhaps the same instrumental music that was played on the bus). It is important that there is an air of something akin to celebration.

When audience members arrive at this space, actors at a reception table meet them. The actors wear labels that say INSIDER. Spectators are asked to line up in rows, in front of individual actors. Each audience member is handed the OUTSIDER card below and is asked to fill their card at the table, while the actor watches over them to answer any queries.

https://doi.org/10.11647/OBP.0223.04

What might be reasons underpinning the particular prompts that OUTSIDERS (spectators) need to complete on their identification badges?

Hint: look into adult learning theories.

OUTSIDER My name is: ——————————. I am a: ————————————. I want to be here because: ————————————	PLEASE KEEP THIS CARD WITH YOU AT ALL TIMES If you need anything over the course of the day, please approach one of the GUIDES for assistance.

Pheran
A type of tunic that is particular to Kashmir

Hijab
Scarf worn by Muslim women

Kurta
A tunic

Dupatta
A type of scarf

Once audience members have finished filling out their individual cards, they are asked to place them in lanyards and to hang the lanyards around their necks at all times. The actors at the table then direct each audience member to an area that is designed to be a green room.

In this green room, with mirrors, other performers wearing INSIDER tags meet the audience members and guide them towards a range of costume items. Some are extremely specific to the context of Kashmir: pherans, hijabs, kurtas, dupattas. Other elements are not so relevant to Kashmir: safari hats and vests, masks, brightly coloured short / sleeveless clothing, clearly ill-conceived clothing vis-à-vis the codes of the local context in which the play is being performed.

Let's say you are creating an immersive experience that seeks to give your audience an insight into income inequality, as it manifests in your local context.

Who would be the target audience?

As each audience member enters this green-room area, they show an actor their OUTSIDER card. The actor reads the card and chooses a costume item that the audience members will have to wear, in addition to their existing clothing, over the course of the day-long journey. The actor can choose the item based on something the spectator has written on their card. The actor can choose the item completely at random. Of course, audience members can choose not to wear the clothing given to them, in which case, something else can be chosen by the INSIDER. Alternatively, the spectators can choose their own costume. However: each audience member must wear a costume item.

While the exact costume item handed to each audience member can be different, what is important is that all *spectators are given — in addition to an individualized costume item — a bag.*

The bags can be of different sizes or colours or shapes, as long as they are big enough to carry the stone souvenirs that are given to them throughout the experience, and have a legible label sewn on them. The label reads:

This bag belongs to

_____

(the name of the OUTSIDER, as on their card, is written here by the actor).

(continued)

What role would you cast the audience in?

What apparatus would you give them to aid in their transformation (masks, costume pieces, and such)?

How do your ideas contend with the ethics of 'becoming' someone else and the potential tokenization that might occur through your choices?

All audience members will have to carry these bags with them over the course of the 24-hour journey. The actors should tell them this. Most bags need to be strong; resilient. Others can be intentionally crafted with less finesse.

While audience members are getting dressed for their journey and are receiving their bags, GUIDES #1 and #2 walk in and begin to meet each spectator informally. They welcome each individual audience member, introduce themselves as the GUIDES, and establish through these informal conversations that the audience members are, in fact, in the "Valley."

Once all the audience members have their OUTSIDER cards, costume item, and bag — and once the GUIDES have met everyone in the group informally — the music fades; all the other actors leave; there is silence.

And in that silence, the GUIDES step forward:

GUIDE #1: Welcome, ladies and gentlemen. Welcome to this "tour." We are —

GUIDE #2: Is "tour" the right word?

GUIDE #1: Isn't it?

GUIDE #2: Sounds so... touristy.

GUIDE #1: *Chalo,* suggest something else, then.

GUIDE #2: "Journey" might be better, no?

GUIDE #1: (*Smiles*). So, let's start again.

Welcome to this journey (*emphasizes the word*), ladies and gentlemen. We are so very glad to have you with us.

The character of GUIDE #2 was included as a strategy of autoethnography.

How do you understand autoethnography?

How do you understand the role of this methodology in *Chronicles from Kashmir*?

This journey… it's something special. Something unique. A journey during which you will become part of a conversation between an ordinary Kashmiri (*points to himself*), and an ordinary non-Kashmiri (*points at GUIDE #2*).

There are no diplomats here; no agencies; no NGOs — just two people from the "inside" and the "outside;" two people who have chosen to come together to explore if, and how, they might be able to walk together.

What is the place for an outsider in the face of our struggles in Kashmir today? This is the question that lies at the heart of this journey.

GUIDE #2: I look at Kashmir through the eyes of guest; a foreigner; an outsider. And today, with the support of my friend here, I will be sharing some of the stories that I have encountered in my journeys through Kashmir.

GUIDE #1: I have heard my friend here speak of these experiences before, but this is the first time that I will be witnessing the stories in this form. This tou — sorry, journey (*both GUIDES smile at each other*) — is as new for me as it is for you…

Hartal
A strike

Aam aadmi and aurat
Common man and woman

Kehewa
A tea preparation that is particular to Kashmir

As someone who has grown up here and has witnessed the highs and lows of Kashmir's struggles, I have always wondered what outsiders experience when they come to my home. Do they simply see the beauty of the land? Or do they only see the *hartals* and the protests and the voices of dissent? Do they speak to the *aam aadmi* and *aurat* and get a sense of what is actually happening here? Or do they only sit on houseboats and drink copious amounts of *kehewa*, oblivious to what's happening around them? I have always wondered what outsiders see when they come to Kashmir…

GUIDE #2: Over the course of the next day, you will walk around different spaces with us. In some of them, you will be asked to watch and listen. In others, you will be invited to become part of the action. In all of them, you have a choice to be involved as much as you wish.

Please always wear your ID cards and please, always carry the bags that have been given to you.

Before we start our journey, are there any questions?

Audience members are given the opportunity to ask the GUIDES questions about practical matters: When will they get to use the toilet? When will they get to eat?

If questions go beyond practicalities to the content or intent of the work, the GUIDES simply smile and say: "We hope you will find an answer to that question over the course of our time together."

When the spectators have asked all their questions, the GUIDES lead them to the next space.

The path to the next space is incredibly pristine; clean; a well-manicured lawn, for instance. Perhaps it even has a lake. There are flowers in full bloom. The GUIDES and the audience stroll through this space; relaxed — taking their time to arrive at the next setting.

If we were to consider audience configurations in theatre (proscenium, thrust, the round) as symbolic elements, what might be the symbolism of using the promenade (where spectators move from one space to another)?

How can the physical placement of an audience in the theatre function as an allegory for the content of the work?

Devise two scenes, about a topic of your choice, which are performed in two different rooms. The audience must be taken from space A to space B, without breaking the world of the performance.

Then, try to stage same two scenes, but this time *without* the movement between spaces i.e., both scenes are performed in the same place, to a static audience.

What changes?

What stays the same?

Scene One: The Experiment

▶ WATCH THE VIDEO

The GUIDES lead the audience into a space. The walls and floors of the space are covered with paper or blackboards. As spectators enter, they see the TEACHER standing alone, writing the same statements over and over again — while simultaneously reading them aloud.

TEACHER: (*reading and writing*) I will not disobey my parents. I will not disobey my teachers. I will not disobey my elders. I will not disobey those in power.

His writing increases in speed, till he is scribbling, talking unintelligibly: fast and rapid. At some point, when the actor playing the TEACHER is tired, he stops. And just looks at his work.

Silence.

The COORDINATOR enters. He brings in the lungs of a goat on a plate. He places it on one of the tables, looks at the TEACHER.

COORDINATOR: Are you ready?

The TEACHER nods.

THE COORDINATOR opens the door and invites the PUPIL to come into the room. The PUPIL stands quietly, entranced by the space and the equipment.

While the COORDINATOR speaks, the TEACHER walks over to the plate with the lungs and starts blowing air into them; over and over again.

COORDINATOR: Ladies and gentlemen: the subject of our experiment is to determine the pedagogical effect of punishment. To what degree does punishment accelerate the learning process? Imagine. If with one slap a child learns to behave, don't we waste years teaching and persuading only with nice words? We don't have time to lose.

> *The Experiment & The Man & the Woman are the two scenes that stay close to Gambaro's versions of them in IFF.*
>
> Compare and contrast these scenes with their Argentinian counterparts, paying particular attention to the elements that have been adapted.

https://doi.org/10.11647/OBP.0223.05

Imagine this: you live in a world where ethical guidelines do not exist.

You are tasked with designing a sociological/ psychological experiment — like the well-known Milgram obedience experiments or the Stanford prison experiment — to understand humans' ability to become complicit within structures of oppression and violence.

What kind of experiment would you conduct?

This is purely a theoretical exercise!

The COORDINATOR begins observing the TEACHER playing with the lungs.

COORDINATOR: Please, sir, stop playing with those lungs!

TEACHER: Okay, okay. I'm sorry. It's so much fun that...

COORDINATOR: Of course, it's fun. Shall we begin?

TEACHER: At your orders, sir!

COORDINATOR: You, sir, will be the teacher.

TEACHER: Yes, delighted.

COORDINATOR: (*turning to the PUPIL and breaking his trance*) You will be the pupil.

PUPIL: I will be the pupil.

The COORDINATOR points the PUPIL toward a curtained off area in the room. The COORDINATOR opens the curtain with great flair and points the PUPIL to a chair that is surrounded by wires. The TEACHER watches this with the utmost interest.

COORDINATOR: Please be seated. Don't be afraid. It's an experiment; remember that.

PUPIL: Happy to please!

COORDINATOR: Take off your jacket, roll up your sleeves. Thank you. We have to strap you in. If you would like to quit...?

PUPIL: No! Absolutely not! I'm really excited to be here.

COORDINATOR: (*Calls to the TEACHER.*) Will you help me?

TEACHER: Yes, of course!

The COORDINATOR takes a tube of cream and starts smearing the PUPIL'S forearms.

COORDINATOR: The cream facilitates the passage of the current and prevents burns. It's an experiment; don't be frightened.

PUPIL: I'm not afraid. I'm not afraid at all. I really am so happy to help.

The COORDINATOR attaches electrodes to the PUPIL'S forearms. The TEACHER helps diligently.

COORDINATOR: How obliging! Thank you.

PUPIL: It's… very tight.

COORDINATOR: Let's loosen this a bit. (*The COORDINATOR loosens the electrodes*) Now, you — the teacher — are going to station yourself over there.

THE COORDINATOR points the TEACHER to one side of the room. This area has a table and chair. On the table is a machine with many, many buttons. From where the TEACHER sits, the PUPIL can only be heard and not seen.

COORDINATOR: (*To the PUPIL*) You. You pay attention. The teacher will read out a list of word-association pairs, such as: day-sun, night-moon, mother-love, and so on. Then, he will repeat a word from one of the pairs and ask you to choose, from four options, the correct word association for it. You must remember which of the four words was associated with day in the original list that the teacher read to you. If you make a mistake, you'll receive an electric shock as punishment. This will help you learn.

PUPIL: Why will punishment teach me?

COORDINATOR: The shock won't be strong.

PUPIL: Never?

COORDINATOR: No! Unless you really blunder. But that's impossible. They're very obvious associations. For idiots.

The COORDINATOR walks over to the TEACHER and hands him a sheet of paper.

COORDINATOR: Here is the list of words. A clean game: read slowly, with good pronunciation.

As the TEACHER gets ready to read the list —

COORDINATOR: Wait! Roll up your sleeve.

TEACHER: Me? What for?

COORDINATOR: I want to give you a charge of forty-five volts.

TEACHER: Me? But, I'm the teacher!

COORDINATOR: Don't be afraid. I'm doing it so that you'll appreciate the intensity of the punishment. Otherwise, you might have a heavy hand.

The COORDINATOR puts an electrode on the TEACHER'S arm, pushes a button. TEACHER gasps.

TEACHER: That's strong!

COORDINATOR: No, no. You'll start with fifteen volts. You won't have to increase it much. Just read. Slowly, and in a clear voice.

TEACHER: Day-sun, night-moon, mother-love, water-ship, plague-war, house-forest, child-innocence, prison-bars, window-freedom, blue-sky, bird-flight, nation-India, torture-dissuasion.

COORDINATOR: Very good! Now you must read one word, then four more, so that the pupil will pick the correct association. If he makes a mistake, say "Error," press the first button, and tell the pupil the voltage with which you're punishing him. Then read the right answer. Punishments start at 15 volts and end at 450 volts. As you see, it couldn't be easier. Begin.

TEACHER: Sun: day, forest, mother, water.

PUPIL: Day!

COORDINATOR: Very good! Let's go on! Do you like it?

TEACHER: Yes! It's terrific!

COORDINATOR: Continue.

TEACHER: Night: plague, forest, moon, child.

PUPIL: Moon!

TEACHER: Correct! This is like a drug!

COORDINATOR: Ssshh! Go on!

TEACHER: Mother: day, water, child, love.

Silence from the PUPIL.

TEACHER: But you know this! What memories do you have of your mother?

COORDINATOR: Now, don't help! It's not scientific!

PUPIL: Chi-

TEACHER: No!

COORDINATOR: Excuse me, sir. This is an experiment, not a game.

PUPIL: We can't repeat?

COORDINATOR: Just this once. You've got to follow the rules.

TEACHER: Just this once, not again. Mother: day, water, child, love. (*Pause*) Well?

PUPIL: Love!

TEACHER: Very good! But you need to answer faster next time. Blue: ship, bird, sky, house. (*Pause*) Come on, I told you —

PUPIL: Could you repeat the question?

TEACHER: No. I'm not allowed to. Answer. I can't wait —

PUPIL: Bird!

TEACHER: (*Looks at the COORDINATOR*) He made a mistake. Now what do I do?

COORDINATOR: The first. Fifteen volts.

TEACHER: (*He looks excitedly at the button*) Here we go!

The PUPIL is jolted but cries out more in surprise than pain.

TEACHER: Come on, that was nothing. You're fine. Let's move on to the next one. Try to remember, ok? Plague: child, innocence, love, night.

COORDINATOR: (*quietly*) You forgot war.

TEACHER: I did?

COORDINATOR: Plague-war. It's all right, let it go. It doesn't matter.

TEACHER: Should I repeat?

The COORDINATOR shrugs.

TEACHER: No. He should know. Come on, pupil. Quick. Otherwise this is boring.

PUPIL: Night.

TEACHER: He made a mistake! Thirty volts!

A louder groan from the PUPIL.

TEACHER: Moving right along. Child: love, mother, innocence, bird.

PUPIL: Love!

TEACHER: He made a mistake! You were dreaming! Forty-five volts!

He pushes another button. Howling loudly, the PUPIL arches his back. Surprised by the howling, the TEACHER looks into the other room. To the COORDINATOR, disturbed.

TEACHER: A bit strong, wasn't it?

COORDINATOR: No. This is a scientific experiment, and I am in charge. What experiment? Just as I told you: simply to determine the effectiveness of punishment in learning. If from the beginning we doubt, we'll never arrive at a conclusion.

TEACHER: Yes, that's right. The associations are easy.

COORDINATOR: And the current is not too bad. I gave you forty-five volts, remember?

TEACHER: Yes! And I didn't shout. What a weakling this student is! Pupil, listen to me. Don't waste your energy screaming. Pay attention to the associations. Sky: mother, child, innocence, blue.

PUPIL: Blue!

TEACHER: Good.

COORDINATOR: Magnificent. See, we're already getting results.

TEACHER: It's no time to stop, then. Plague: prison, house, forest, war.

PUPIL mumbles something unintelligible.

TEACHER: What? Repeat? I can't... (*he looks at the COORDINATOR, and speaks in a quieter tone*) Sir, can I repeat? Just this once? He's not very intelligent.

The COORDINATOR shrugs.

TEACHER: Listen. This is the last time I'm going to repeat something ok? Don't let your mind wander. Plague: prison, house, forest, war.

PUPIL: Prison.

TEACHER: God; he's an idiot!

COORDINATOR: Teacher, all you need to do is say, "Error," and press the button. That is your job. There's no need for the commentary.

TEACHER rolls his eyes at the COORDINATOR and presses a button.

PUPIL: No, no! I didn't think it would be so painful.

TEACHER: Pupil, pay attention. You think I like pushing these little buttons? Try to remember. Blue: bird, flight, sky, freedom. Out with it!

PUPIL: I don't remember!

TEACHER: How can you not remember?

PUPIL: I don't!

TEACHER: If you don't remember, take this.

TEACHER presses a button.

PUPIL: (*a scream*) Sky!

TEACHER: Very good! You see? With a little determination, you got it. Okay! Here we go. Flight: bird, blue, forest, night. You have to be quick now. Answer.

PUPIL: I won't play. No matter what you say.

COORDINATOR: Youth today! Now he refuses.

TEACHER: What's the matter with him? Should we let him go?

COORDINATOR: You heard him agree to be part of this. He can't give up now. The results are important, aren't they? I know you can be counted on.

TEACHER: Pupil? Pay attention.

PUPIL: Go to hell! Let's change places!

TEACHER: Change places? That's crazy. It'll be worse for you, if you don't answer. Bird: flight, blue, plague, war. You see how I'm trying to help you? I'm repeating the words, and that isn't even allowed. Answer!

PUPIL: I'll make a mistake!

TEACHER: Answer! (*He pushes a button*)

PUPIL screams louder. TEACHER looks at the COORDINATOR.

TEACHER: He's screaming.

COORDINATOR: He feels a bit jolted. You're doing great. You have just one thing to watch out for: 450 volts. Otherwise, after a week, there isn't a mark.

TEACHER nods.

TEACHER: Pupil. Listen carefully. Are you listening?

PUPIL: Are you listening?

TEACHER: We'll see who's listening. Bird: night, flight, house, plague.

PUPIL: I don't remember!

TEACHER: Don't be such an ass!

PUPIL: Don't be such an ass! Plague!

TEACHER: Imbecile! Bird-plague! See how he answers! He's jerking me around!

The COORDINATOR pushes a button. The PUPIL screams, weeps.

TEACHER: And now he's crying. Listen, kid, answer right, or I'll blow you away. Window: prison, flight, torture, freedom.

PUPIL: Torture! Torture!

TEACHER: What did you say? Teacher? Idiot! You're making fun of me!

He pushes the button. The PUPIL howls.

COORDINATOR: One hundred eighty volts. It's moving right along.

PUPIL: LET ME GO. YOU'RE HURTING ME.

Suddenly less sure of himself, the TEACHER speaks in hushed voices to the COORDINATOR.

TEACHER: Do we stop?

COORDINATOR: No.

TEACHER: He doesn't remember anything!

COORDINATOR: He'll remember now.

TEACHER: You think so? He's crying. Screaming. If he's not even answering the questions, isn't this useless?

COORDINATOR: Never! What will be useless is if we don't succeed in getting concrete results after all of this. You have to continue.

TEACHER: I do?

COORDINATOR: Of course. Think about it. Don't you have to complete your task?

TEACHER: Yes... yes. Yes. Of course. Any task that is undertaken should be completed.

COORDINATOR: I can see that you have been taught well.

TEACHER smiles and gets ready to question the PUPIL again.

TEACHER: All right, pupil. We're going to continue now. You need to learn. Nation: prison, bars, India, torture.

PUPIL: I DON'T KNOW.

TEACHER: Shall I press the button?

PUPIL: KASHMIR.

TEACHER: India, idiot!

He pushes the button. The PUPIL howls.

TEACHER: Prison: nation, plague, war, bars.

PUPIL: I DON'T KNOW. LET ME GO. I want to go home.

TEACHER: ANSWER ME.

PUPIL: KASHMIR!

TEACHER: Wrong again.

TEACHER pushes button after button. The PUPIL's screams keep getting louder with each button; he starts convulsing.

COORDINATOR: (*in a hushed voice*) Slow down, now. Only press one button at a time.

TEACHER: Why doesn't he answer right?

COORDINATOR: Teach him. Like you were taught.

TEACHER: Pupil, I don't like doing this to you. Is that clear? You agreed to do this and now you need to concentrate. Ok? Are you ready for the next question? Pupil. I'm reading the next question. You better be ready.

PUPIL: Vultures fly near...

TEACHER: Moon: night, prison, window, flight. This one is easy.

   (*Pause. TEACHER speaks, in a hushed voice to the COORDINATOR.*)

   Sir, there's only the last button left now. 450 volts. If he doesn't answer this question, what do I do?

COORDINATOR shrugs. The TEACHER puts his hand on the last button. Closes his eyes.

TEACHER: He doesn't answer. Why doesn't he answer? Pupil. Answer me. Moon.

PUPIL: Ni — Niiight.

TEACHER: He made a mistake. He made a mistake... again. It's deliberate. He can't not know the answer. It hurts me to do this —

He pushes the last button. Silence.

TEACHER: He didn't scream.

COORDINATOR: Very good! 450 volts! Excellent! Your help has been invaluable.

TEACHER: Why didn't he help?

COORDINATOR: Look... we choose the risks we take. Sometimes we're not so lucky.

TEACHER: It was his fault. Wasn't it?

COORDINATOR: Yes, yes. Your work was magnificent!

TEACHER: He didn't even make an effort. A baby at the breast could have answered right.

COORDINATOR: Yes, yes! You were splendid.

COORDINATOR shakes the TEACHER's hand.

COORDINATOR: Thank you ever so much. Don't worry. This was an unforgettable performance.

TEACHER: It was nothing. I did what I could!

COORDINATOR: No, no, you were quick, concise, sure. Thanks ever so much!

The COORDINATOR exits; the PUPIL remains limp in his chair. Silence. The TEACHER remains seated.

After a few seconds, the TEACHER slowly rises from his chair. He walks over to the PUPIL who is lying, silent, with his eyes closed. The TEACHER goes back to the papers/blackboards covering the room, erases what was written there before, and starts writing new lines while reading them aloud. There is something mechanical — robotic — in how the TEACHER does this. The frenzy and chaos of his writing at the beginning of the scene has ceased.

TEACHER: I will not press the button. I will not press the button. I will not press the button. I will not press the button...

Eventually, though, he cannot seem to write anymore. His rhythm is slow and keeps slowing down till he eventually stops.

His numbed gaze lands on the goat lungs. He walks over to them, picks up the lungs, and begins to blow air into them. He watches the lungs carefully. He watches the lungs expand and contract. Expand and contract. Eventually, he blows too much air into them. So much air that the lungs burst, leaving their debris all over his body. He looks at what he is covered in and robotically — mechanically — cleans himself.

The COORDINATOR opens the door. He looks at the TEACHER.

COORDINATOR: Are you ready for the next student?

TEACHER: No. I want to say no.

Pause.

TEACHER: Can I say no?

COORDINATOR: There's only one way to find out.

TEACHER: If I say no, what will you do to me?

COORDINATOR: There's only one way to find out.

TEACHER: I want to say no. I don't want to do this again.

COORDINATOR: Why?

TEACHER: Why?

COORDINATOR: Why do you not want to do this again?

TEACHER: Look at him.

They both look at the PUPIL who is still lying slumped in the chair.

COORDINATOR: And...?

TEACHER: We did that to him!

COORDINATOR: We?

TEACHER: I. I did that to him.

COORDINATOR: Did you? Didn't he do it to himself?

TEACHER: What do you mean?

COORDINATOR: Wasn't it his fault? Wasn't he the one who got the answers wrong?

TEACHER: I pressed the buttons. You made me press the buttons.

COORDINATOR: You could have left at any time.

TEACHER: But you said — you said —

COORDINATOR: What did I say?

TEACHER: That it was for the sake of science.

COORDINATOR: And that it is. It is for the sake of science.

TEACHER: We killed someone for the sake of science?

COORDINATOR: We need to understand how human nature works. We need to understand the role that discipline and punishment play in learning. This student has taken us one step forward in our desire to understand humanity.

TEACHER: And what have we understood from this student?

COORDINATOR: Isn't the answer to that question obvious?

TEACHER: It's not. It's not obvious to me.

COORDINATOR: Then there is nothing left for me to say.

> Who/what are the different entities that the COORDINATOR, TEACHER, PUPIL, and BOSS might symbolize in the Kashmiri context?

Pause.

TEACHER: I don't want to do this again. I want to say no.

The BOSS enters.

BOSS: I hear he doesn't want to do this anymore?

TEACHER: Who is this?

COORDINATOR: Anyone who wants to leave this experiment needs to speak to the Boss. This is the Boss.

A long and uncomfortable silence while the BOSS walks around the room, examines the PUPIL, and then the TEACHER.

BOSS: So, you don't want to participate anymore?

TEACHER: Sir, it's just... I'm sorry to disappoint you...

BOSS: Disappoint? No, no, you are not disappointing me at all. This is actually what we expected would happen.

TEACHER: You expected me to say no?

BOSS: From what we read in your files, we knew that you would have a difficult time following the protocol of the experiment. Isn't that right, Mr. Coordinator?

COORDINATOR: Absolutely, sir.

TEACHER: What files? What did you read about me?

BOSS: Oh, you know, this and that. Anyway, you are sure you want to leave this experiment, correct?

TEACHER: Yes, but... what's in my files?

BOSS: They are your files, son. You should know what's in there. Isn't that right, Mr. Coordinator?

COORDINATOR: Absolutely, sir. It's your life that's in the files, Mr. Teacher. You know what you've done.

TEACHER: What does that mean? I haven't done anything.

BOSS: Then I guess we have nothing in our files.

BOSS and COORDINATOR share a laugh.

TEACHER: I, uh... I don't understand what's happening here.

BOSS: It's a simple decision, son. Are you going to continue the experiment or not?

TEACHER: I want to say no.

BOSS and COORDINATOR look at each other.

COORDINATOR: In that case, we need you to come with us and take care of some paperwork.

TEACHER: You want me to go with you?

COORDINATOR: Yes.

TEACHER: Alone?

BOSS: Well, we'll be there with you.

BOSS and COORDINATOR laugh.

TEACHER: Where will you take me?

COORDINATOR: There's only one way to find out!

TEACHER: Am I going to be punished for saying no?

BOSS: Punished?! You are the teacher, aren't you?

TEACHER: So, I can leave after we take care of the paperwork?

COORDINATOR: We just need you to come with us.

The TEACHER leaves nervously with the BOSS and COORDINATOR who each have a hold on one of his arms. The PUPIL remains slumped on the chair.

> Stone souvenirs are handed to spectators at the end of each section in *Chronicles from Kashmir*.
>
> How do you understand the significance of the stones in this performance?
>
> How do you interpret the use of intertextuality *vis-à-vis* the stones — both as an aesthetic strategy, and as a pedagogical tool?

A moment of silence.

During the conversation that follows, the GUIDES — slowly — take stones that have been placed in some part of the space and hand one stone to each audience member. The spectators are invited — via the GUIDES' gestures — to place the stones given to them inside the bags they were given when they arrived. The stones are their souvenirs.

Stone souvenirs are handed to audience members at multiple points in Chronicles from Kashmir, *and in each instance, the stones can be slightly different from each other: different sizes, shapes, colours. All that is essential is that the souvenir is a stone. Or something like it. Something like a stone that will increase the weight that an audience member has to carry in their bag.*

Every single stone souvenir that a spectator gets during their journey is somehow embellished with a piece of paper that is glued/tied/painted/creatively embedded onto it. This piece of paper is intended to be a keepsake, of sorts; a keepsake that the audience can choose to engage with after their journey through Chronicles from Kashmir *has ended. Each time a stone souvenir is given to spectators, therefore, there is a description in the script of what the stone might be embellished with. In this scene, the stone that the GUIDES give each spectator contains the information about the Milgram experiment* (something like McLeod, 2007).

So, as they speak the lines below, the GUIDES hand a stone souvenir to each audience member and silently invite them to place the object in their bags.

GUIDE #1: So, you said at the beginning that you were going to show us an outsider's experiences of Kashmir, yes?

GUIDE #2: Yes.

GUIDE #1: So, this story that you've shown us, you've witnessed this in Kashmir?

GUIDE #2: No, no. Not all the stories that I'm showing you are direct representations… It's just that something about what you saw here reminds me of things that I've seen and heard in Kashmir.

GUIDE #1: So, what was it about this story that reminded you of Kashmir?

GUIDE #2 smiles.

GUIDE #2: Come on, sir. That would be too easy! You tell me — was there something in this story that, to you, seems linked to Kashmir?

GUIDE#1: I think… I think you are asking an important question: how do ordinary people become each other's torturers and murderers? How do ordinary people, like this teacher, like you and me, like the others here, become part of something dangerous and violent? How do we become complicit with acts of violence even though we are not the masterminds like Hitler? How does this happen? ... Am I right?

GUIDE #2: Possibly. (*He smiles mischievously.*)

GUIDE #1: Possibly?!

GUIDE #2: *Arre*, sir. This is not a test — I can't just tell if you got something right or wrong! The interpretations of what I share are up to you; the interpretations are in all of your hands.

> *Arre*
> Hey

GUIDE #1: OK if you won't answer my question, let me ask you something. What kind of teacher do you think you would have been in that situation?

GUDE #2: If I had to press those buttons, you mean?

GUIDE #1: Yes.

GUIDE #2: I think... I would like to think that I would have said no from the beginning.

GUIDE #1: And if they had threatened to kill you if you refused?

GUDE #2: I would have still said no.

GUIDE #1: What if they had threatened to kill the student if you didn't do what you were told?

GUDE #2: If the experiment was going to kill him anyway, would it make a difference if they killed him before I did? I mean, at least he would die knowing that I refused to harm him, no?

GUIDE #1: What good is that knowledge to him if he's dead?

Pause.

> What are your thoughts on the exchanges that occur between the GUIDES before/during/after each scene?
>
> Does their dialogue serve as necessary framing?
>
> Or does it belabour points that are already obvious?
>
> Are there some audiences for whom such explicit framing might be necessary, versus others for whom ambiguity would be preferred?
>
> What factors might influence/determine such shifts in strategy?

GUIDE #1: Let's make it more complicated... Now imagine that they threatened one of your loved ones if you didn't participate in the experiment. Then would you refuse?

Slight pause.

GUIDE #2: I would want to protect the person I loved.

GUIDE #1: Yes.

GUIDE #2: But I still wouldn't want to participate in something like that.

GUIDE #1: So?

GUIDE #2: So... I have no idea what I would do.

GUIDE #1 smiles.

GUIDE #1: So, Kashmir has taught you that —

GUIDE #2: — that it is not always easy to understand why people do what they do. Our own acts of complicity that —

GUIDE #1: — that are powerful and powerless at the same time?

GUIDE #2: Yes.

GUIDE #1: Yes.

Pause. They look around at the audience.

GUIDE #2: *Chalo*, what are you going to share with us next?

GUIDE #1: Please, follow me.

As audience members exit this space and move on to the next one, they walk down a path that is covered in/composed of electrical wires. As they walk between spaces during Chronicles from Kashmir, *the GUIDES are welcome to informally interact with audience members.*

That said, there doesn't always have to be conversation.

The paths are liminal spaces between one narrative and the next.
They are grey zones.
Where everything is murky.
And revels in being that way.

Scene Two: The Departure

[QR code] ▶ WATCH THE VIDEO

The GUIDES lead the audience into a kitchen; NEIGHBOURS #1, #2, & #3 enter with the them.

DOCTOR: Good day everyone.

GUIDE: Good day!

NEIGHBOUR #1: Hello! How's it going, doctor?

The three NEIGHBOURS shake hands with the DOCTOR. The DOCTOR shakes hands with spectators, informally greeting them to his home. The GUIDES direct spectators where to sit. Once everyone is seated:

DOCTOR: I'm really glad to see you all and to have you here as part of your journey. Tell me about your trip to Kashmir so far — what have you seen, what have you learned?

The audience is given a chance to interact with the DOCTOR. The GUIDES encourage the audience to speak: to establish that, indeed, there are occasions when spectators can directly engage with the performers. Whatever the response is from the audience, the DOCTOR engages with questions that invite spectators to clarify their thoughts and opinions. When a rapport has been established:

DOCTOR: Listen, I would love to offer you all something to eat... But it's been a slightly difficult time and I don't really have anything at the moment.

NEIGHBOUR #3: What's wrong Doctor *saab*?

DOCTOR: Oh, you know what's been happening around here. I found a note on the door yesterday... The same kind of note that Kaul *saab* received.

> *Saab*
> Sir

https://doi.org/10.11647/OBP.0223.06

NEIGHBOUR #3: Who was the note from?

DOCTOR: Well, we'll never know who they're from exactly... Could be some kids playing a prank, could be something more serious.

NEIGHBOUR #2: What are you going to do?

DOCTOR: I'm thinking of publishing the note in the paper tomorrow, so that people can see what happened. And if it is some kids having their fun, they can be stopped.

NEIGHBOUR #1: It might not be kids you know... It might be something more serious.

DOCTOR: I know.

NEIGHBOUR #1: And by publishing the note in the paper you will only draw more attention to yourself.

DOCTOR: I know that.

NEIGHBOUR #1: So?

DOCTOR: What else can I do?

NEIGHBOUR #3: Look I think you're right. Publish it in the paper and if anything happens, we are with you.

> *Janab*
> Your Excellency
> (a colloquialism that is used to connote respect, regardless of the gender of the person being addressed)

NEIGHBOUR #1: Please, *janab*. Don't make glib promises that you cannot keep. If this note is from who we think it's from, and if Tickoo *saab* publishes it in the newspaper, there is nothing we can do to protect him from them. I'm sorry, Doctor *saab*. I'm not trying to upset you, but the truth is that if they show up in the neighbourhood because you publish their note in the newspaper, you cannot expect us to come out to save you.

NEIGHBOUR #3: I'll come out.

NEIGHBOUR #2: Much good you'll do, standing outside his door on your own. They'll just take you down with him.

DOCTOR: Please, don't get involved in this any of you. I don't want anything to happen to you. I just need to figure out what I'm going to do.

NEIGHBOUR #1: I've heard that the Pandits in the other neighbourhood have already left.

DOCTOR: Yes, I've heard the same thing.

NEIGHBOUR #3: But there are others like you Doctor s*aab,* who are still here. So, don't feel pressured to leave. Take your time and make a decision that you're comfortable with.

NEIGHBOUR #2: Time? You think there is time to make this decision? Doctor *saab,* you need to decide quickly. Things are going from bad to worse every day.

DOCTOR: I know that... I know. I'll try to decide by tonight. There's a bus leaving first thing tomorrow morning and...

MAN enters. The lines below overlap. There is a sense of chaos. Of fear. Of unrest.

MAN: Let me through!

DOCTOR: Excuse me.

MAN: You. You're the one we've been looking for —

NEIGHBOUR #3: What's going on? Hey! Let him go! What the hell is going on?

NEIGHBOUR #3 tries to defend the DOCTOR. NEIGHBOURS #1 and #2 quietly leave the room.

DOCTOR: Let me go!

The DOCTOR pushes the MAN; NEIGHBOUR #3 tries to help him by beating the MAN with a broom. Confusion.

NEIGHBOUR #3: Let him go! Let him go!

The OFFICIAL enters.

OFFICIAL: What's going on here? Halt! Separate!

DOCTOR,
MAN,
NEIGHBOUR #3: (*all at the same time*) Sir, they were pushing him! — Over here — Over there — They tied him up — They dragged him down —

OFFICIAL: One at a time.

NEIGHBOUR #3: Sir, what is happening here? He's a good man.

OFFICIAL: It doesn't matter what you think.

NEIGHBOUR #3: But we saw...!

OFFICIAL: What you saw is of no consequence.

NEIGHBOUR #3 mixes in with the audience. The OFFICIAL moves off to the side, crosses his arms, his expression serious. MAN has DOCTOR down on his knees and keeps him kneeling if he ever tries to rise. Throughout the following interrogation, the OFFICIAL walks around the kitchen — tipping over containers, spilling staples and spices everywhere. The room should be in complete disarray by the time the OFFICIAL exits: a mix of food and smells and memories.

OFFICIAL: Name.

DOCTOR: Tickoo.

OFFICIAL: Tickoo?

MAN: Sir, this is Sanjay Tickoo and is one of the men that we have been looking for. He stands accused of not having done enough to promote equal educational opportunities in this community.

OFFICIAL: Ah, yes. He is one of those people.

DOCTOR: Sir, I haven't done anything. Please, sir. I don't know what he is talking about. Why are you doing this to me?

OFFICIAL: Silence. I'll ask the questions here.

Silence.

OFFICIAL: How long have you lived here?

DOCTOR: My family has lived here for generations, sir.

OFFICIAL: How many generations exactly?

DOCTOR: I'm not sure, sir. At least four or five. Hundred. Maybe more...

OFFICIAL: I see. Tell me about your family.

DOCTOR: What would you like to know, sir?

OFFICIAL: What do they do?

DOCTOR: Sir, we are a family of doctors. My grandparents, parents, myself, we are all doctors. My brother is a lawyer. My sister is a homemaker, and she lives in Delhi.

OFFICIAL: Delhi, I see. I suppose that's to be expected.

DOCTOR: I don't know what you mean, sir. She's married there and —

OFFICIAL: Yes, yes. I know why she's in Delhi rather than Srinagar or Lahore.

DOCTOR: I... I don't know what you mean, sir.

OFFICIAL: And your brother? Where is he?

DOCTOR: Right now, he is on a business trip in London, sir.

OFFICIAL: London, huh. It must be nice to have so many opportunities.

DOCTOR: Everything we have, we have had to earn, sir. We have worked hard for what we have.

OFFICIAL: How do you give back to your neighbourhood?

> What are the complex ways in which complicity manifests? Where does the responsibility of relative privilege begin/end?

DOCTOR: My neigh — what do you mean, sir?

OFFICIAL: Your family is doing well. How do you share your wealth and opportunity with those around you, who might not have as much as you?

Pause. OFFICIAL smirks at the DOCTOR's visible confusion.

OFFICIAL: *Chalo*, let's talk about the school in this neighbourhood. Your family's school.

DOCTOR: What about the school, sir?

OFFICIAL: Tell me something. Who are the students in the school?

DOCTOR: They are all from here, sir.

OFFICIAL: Don't try to evade the question. Isn't the school that you and your family studied in, the school that your great grandfather established, the 'best' school in this neighbourhood, only for your community's children?

DOCTOR: No, sir. It's for everyone. Everyone is welcome at our school — wherever they are from.

OFFICIAL: Oh, is that right? And you make sure there is equal access for all the children in this *mohalla* to go to your school?

> *Mohalla*
> Neighborhood

DOCTOR: I... I don't understand, sir. I don't stop anyone's children from going to any school.

OFFICIAL: Let me rephrase my question. Do you make a conscious effort to ensure that children from outside your community have access to your school?

DOCTOR: I —

OFFICIAL: You are on the board of the school, correct?

DOCTOR: Yes, sir, I'm on the school board because my great-grandfather started the school. I still don't understand what you want from me.

OFFICIAL: I want you to admit your part in the inequality that has been created in this neighbourhood and in Kashmir.

DOCTOR: What?

OFFICIAL: I. Want. You. To. Admit. It.

DOCTOR: Admit what, sir?

OFFICIAL: Admit your part in the inequality that exists between your community and mine.

DOCTOR: Sir, I'm just on the board of the school. I don't decide who attends the school.

OFFICIAL: But do you do your part, as a citizen of Kashmir, to make sure that the school treats everyone fairly? Do you make sure that other people's children can go there too; not just your own?

DOCTOR: I don't know what I'm expected to say, sir... I don't understand.

OFFICIAL: Of course, you don't understand. In your opinion, you are just one person, right? The inequality that exists between your community and ours, is not your fault? Let me tell you something, Mr. Tickoo. The inequality in Kashmir is, in some way, the fault of everyone in your community. Do you understand what I'm saying to you, Doctor *saab*?

A long silence.

> Consider an instance in your life when you were/ are complicit with a situation of injustice.
>
> If you were to be on trial for this complicity, who would be your defence? Your prosecution? Your jury?

DOCTOR: (*Quietly*) Some Kashmiris have more than other Kashmiris because of... because of one reason or another.

(*Building intensity*) But I still do not understand how any of this is my fault, sir. I don't know what you expect me to do about the situation of the school. I don't know what you expect me to do about the circumstances that I was born into. Yes, I'm on the board of the school and help with school activities sometimes. But I am, first and foremost, a doctor. And as a doctor, I treat all my patients fairly; regardless of which community they belong to.

NEIGHBOUR #3: Sir, that's true. Doctor *saab* always —

OFFICIAL gives NEIGHBOUR #3 a look that immediately silences them.

OFFICIAL: Let me ask you this, Mr. Tickoo, if everyone in Kashmir were to think like you: that some people just have more privilege and there is nothing to be done about it, will anything change?

> Look into the narratives surrounding the Kashmiri Pandit community.

DOCTOR: I don't know, sir. But how does blaming me for a system that I had no part in creating change anything either? I don't understand what you want from me.

OFFICIAL: You don't understand... That's the problem, isn't it, Mr. Tickoo? You do not understand your role in what's happening in Kashmir these days. That's why you are receiving these notes that tell you to leave.

Pause.

DOCTOR: You know about the notes.

OFFICIAL: We know everything, Doctor *saab*.

DOCTOR: So, it's not some children playing a joke on me?

OFFICIAL: No.

DOCTOR: The notes are real?

OFFICIAL: Yes.

DOCTOR: You want me to leave Kashmir?

OFFICIAL: Well, I wouldn't say *I* want you to leave Kashmir specifically. But it is advised that you leave.

DOCTOR: Sir, this is my home.

OFFICIAL: If it were your home, don't you think you would do more to address the inequalities here?

DOCTOR: No, no. This isn't right, sir. I am free to stay here if I wish.

MAN and OFFICIAL laugh.

DOCTOR: Am I not free?

> The role of the OFFICIAL in this scene has been intentionally written as being ambiguous. Based on your research and understanding of what is happening/has happened to Kashmiri Pandits, who might this archetype represent?

OFFICIAL: You can stay if you like. But... we cannot be held responsible if anything happens to you. Consider this conversation your final warning.

OFFICIAL and MAN exit. Silence.

> In the process of creating *Chronicles from Kashmir,* the choice of cultural elements — like the song at the end of the scene — was left to the members of EKTA.
>
> If you were to stage this work in your context, how would you go about identifying these pieces of the puzzle? Who would you contact? How would you begin this process?

NEIGHBOUR #3 stands up and goes to the DOCTOR. They hug. NEIGHBOUR #3 exits.

The DOCTOR stops being able to see the audience members and the GUIDES. He is in his own world. He stares at a trunk, which has been placed in the middle of the room. He stares at the trunk and after a few seconds, makes a decision. He walks swiftly around the room, collecting objects that have meaning for him, placing each of them on the trunk: the items are somehow symbolic of Kashmir.

Finally, the DOCTOR's glance lands on the pheran *— a traditional Kashmiri tunic — that he is wearing. He removes it violently and throws it on the floor. As soon as it hits the floor, he runs to it, picks up the* pheran, *hugs it. He looks at all the objects that he has placed on the trunk. He takes an object or two in his hands, because he cannot take everything with him, no? Some objects fall to the ground when he opens the trunk. He gazes at the fallen objects and at the objects in his hands. He climbs into the trunk with the objects in his hands. He closes the trunk.*

Silence.

GUIDE #1 breaks out into song — a song associated with exodus; with migration. A few lines into the song, GUIDE #2 hands stone souvenirs to the audience to place in their bags. Meanwhile, GUIDE #1 continues to sing and the DOCTOR remains inside the trunk. Here, the stone souvenir for the spectator is embellished, somehow, with an image of a long line of migrants/refugees who are en route from one place to another.

> *Topi*
> A hat that functions as a marker of one's identity

When GUIDE #1 finishes his song of lament, the audience is led to the next space down a path that is varyingly draped with hats; hats worn specifically by Kashmiri Pandits — Pandit topis *as they are called.*

Scene Three: The Man & the Woman

 WATCH THE VIDEO

The GUIDES lead everyone to a toilet. A tap drips.

MAN: Why didn't you dry yourself? You're getting the floor all wet.

The WOMAN shivers with cold. The MAN takes off his jacket, puts it on her shoulders. The WOMAN looks at it, wraps herself in the jacket.

MAN: Why didn't you dry yourself? Wasn't there a towel?

WOMAN: No.

MAN: What a mess! They fill the tub but don't put out any towels. What about the water? Was it warm? ...

Pause.

MAN: Was it warm?

WOMAN: No.

MAN pulls a pistol from his belt and cleans it with a rag. He shows the WOMAN his weapon.

MAN: Do you like it? It isn't loaded.

Pause.

MAN: Why so sad?

MAN looks at the audience.

> Who are the MAN and the WOMAN in this scenario?
>
> Who/what might they represent in the context of Kashmir's conflicts?

https://doi.org/10.11647/OBP.0223.07

MAN: Look, there are lots of people. They're watching us... Nothing will happen to you.

Pause.

MAN: You're not pretty with your hair all short like this. But that's not too serious...

Pause.

MAN: Tell me, do you cut your hair?

Pause.

MAN: You're getting my jacket all wet. Sorry, it's the only one I have...

MAN takes the jacket gently, shakes it, and puts it on. With a shiver.

MAN: It's damp... Do you want it? (he *points to the pistol*)

WOMAN: No.

MAN: I'm leaving it for you. I have another. The jacket I can't, it's the only one I have, and I need it. Here

He places the pistol at the WOMANS's feet and takes the jacket. She jumps in fright.

MAN: Take it.

WOMAN: No. I don't want to.

Pause.

MAN: Why are you squeezing your legs together? Do you want to go to the bathroom?

WOMAN: Yes.

MAN: Then go!

WOMAN: They're... watching me.

MAN: So? We're all adults, aren't we? At least they are watching.

Pause. MAN watches the WOMAN staring in one direction.

MAN: What are you doing, always looking over there? What do you see that's so pretty?

MAN puts his cheek against hers. Looks in the same direction. WOMAN flinches.

MAN: I like to see people's eyes when I talk to them... Look at me.

Pause.

MAN: Look. At. Me.

He caresses her with the pistol. She looks at him. MAN gestures to the pistol.

MAN: Do you want it?

WOMAN: No, no! Leave me alone!

Pause.

MAN: Would you like some different clothes?

WOMAN: No.

MAN: Always no! Why? My intentions are good. Don't you get bored all alone?

Pause. He kicks the pistol toward her.

MAN: Take it, it doesn't bite. But don't squeeze the trigger. Unless...

WOMAN: Unless...

MAN: If you squeeze, it's all over.

Pause.

MAN: Do you have a husband?

WOMAN: No.

MAN: Well, then? Take it!

Pause.

MAN: I'm leaving it here, on the floor. All you have to do is lean down.

WOMAN: I don't want... anything.

MAN: I just don't want you to suffer.

WOMAN: No.

MAN: Of course, no.

Pause.

MAN: There's a sun outside. It's hot as hell. So, you don't have a husband? Pity... I'll going to tell them to heat the water up for you.

MAN goes out. The WOMAN looks at the pistol on the floor, leans down, trembling, stretches her hand. Freezes in the act. Silence.

The WOMAN eventually picks up the gun. She thinks. She leaves the room with the gun.

A few seconds later, we hear chains clanking outside the door. The WOMAN walks back in. She is holding the chains in her hands. She is wearing a coat. The MAN is tied up in chains. The WOMAN drags him in and fastens the chain to a pipe or the toilet bowl or a door, whatever best fits the space.

> What are the different ways to understand the significance of water in this scene?

There are buckets all around the toilet that have been filled with cold water. Or maybe there's a hose in the space. Or maybe there's a hand shower. Using whatever implements are available, the WOMAN douses the MAN in cold water. The process is long. Arduous. Till they are both visibly exhausted by the process.

The WOMAN watches the MAN for a few long moments.

WOMAN: You're getting the floor all wet.

Pause.

WOMAN: Why so sad?

Pause.

WOMAN: Do you know why you're here?

MAN: No.

WOMAN: You don't know?

MAN: No.

WOMAN: You don't recognize me?

MAN: No.

WOMAN smiles. She pulls out the gun. She caresses the MAN's face with the gun. She puts the gun in front of him, the way he did to her.

WOMAN: It'll come to you.

Silence. A flash of recognition.

WOMAN: Now you remember, don't you?

MAN: Look — I know — I'm sorry for what happened to —

WOMAN: You're sorry?

MAN: Yes.

WOMAN: For what?

MAN: For what happened the last time we met.

WOMAN: So, you do remember.

MAN: You were the woman we took from the house.

WOMAN: No.

MAN: The woman we took from the shop.

WOMAN: No.

MAN: The woman we took from the street.

WOMAN: There have been so many of us, have there?

MAN: The bus?

    The hotel?

    The market?

    The river?

    The school?

The WOMAN sits in front of the MAN.

MAN: You're the woman we took from the school.

Silence.

WOMAN: Why did you come to the school that day?

Silence.

WOMAN: Do you have a wife?

MAN: No.

WOMAN: A sister?

MAN: No.

WOMAN: You have a mother.

Silence.

> What are the various gender dynamics that are at play in this scene?
>
> How do these dynamics get muddled when the WOMAN is portrayed by a male actor (as in the video)?

WOMAN: Imagine this. Your mother is in a place where she feels safe. She is in a place where she does her best to move beyond the chaos around her. A place where she is happy.

And then, one day, some men come to that place. They rip it apart. They break down the walls. They tear up the floors.

They take your mother to places that... places that no woman, no person, should ever have to go to.

The men, some of them have their reasons. Some of them don't. They take your mother because they can take her. Because they have the power to take her. Because they are men, after all. Those men can take your mother wherever and whenever they want. And there is nothing that she can do about.

After all, she is a woman. After all, this is a war...

Your mother comes back a different person. She is never the same again. No place is safe for her anymore.

What do you tell that mother?

Silence.

WOMAN: What do you tell that mother?

Silence.

WOMAN: What do you tell that mother?

Getting no response, the WOMAN goes close to the MAN. She jabs at him with the pistol. Slaps him around. Still getting no answer, she puts the gun down and grabs his collar, shaking him till he responds.

WOMAN: What do you tell that mother?

What do you tell that mother?

What do you tell that mother?

What do you tell that mother?

What do you tell that mother?

WHAT DO YOU TELL THAT —

MAN: I TELL HER THAT SHE'S A WOMAN AND SHE HAS TO DEAL WITH IT.

Silence. The WOMAN smiles.

WOMAN: You tell her she's a woman, and she has to deal with it.

MAN: Yes.

Long silence.

WOMAN: I think I'm going to kill you.

MAN: Maybe you should.

WOMAN: Maybe I should.

MAN: But.

WOMAN: But?

MAN: That would make you become like me.

WOMAN: Who says I am not already like you?

MAN: Don't you want to be better?

WOMAN: In this context, to become more like you is to be better.

Silence.

MAN: What are you going to do to me?

She throws a pile of women's clothes in front of the MAN.

WOMAN: I want you to put those on.

MAN hesitates. The WOMAN picks up the gun. The MAN starts to dress himself in women's clothes. He stands there, in the middle of the toilet an absurd figure, in women's clothes and in chains. The WOMAN watches him carefully.

WOMAN: Sit down.

The MAN sits down again. The WOMAN gives him a chore to complete: she puts a bucket of flour and water in front of the MAN.

> *Rotis*
> A kind of bread

WOMAN: I want you to make ro*tis*.

The MAN hesitates. He begins to knead the dough and flour. The WOMAN watches him do this.

WOMAN: My father didn't know how to boil water. If my mother went somewhere for a day, he couldn't eat. He was so... helpless. But the arrogance of that man. He masked his helplessness with arrogance. He pushed her around. He used her. He loved her. But he pushed her around. And the funny thing is, she thought it was the most normal thing in the world. For him to be helplessly arrogant and for her to allow him to carry on that charade... My father didn't know how to boil water.

MAN: So, this is your revenge? To demean me the way your father demeaned your mother.

WOMAN: You find this demeaning? To be dressed as a woman and to make *rotis?*

Pause.

WOMAN: Tell me about your parents. What were they like?

MAN: Same as yours, I guess. My mother ran the home and my father —

WOMAN: Ran her?

Pause.

WOMAN: And?

MAN: And?

Silence.

WOMAN: How many women did you bring to this place? A hundred? Two hundred? Five hundred? More?

MAN: I don't remember.

WOMAN: And the way you treated these women, was it the way your father treated your mother?

MAN: Those are completely different things.

WOMAN: Are they?

MAN: Yes. This is a war.

WOMAN: So is marriage, for many people...

Pause.

WOMAN: So? How did you treat those women?

MAN: I tried to be gentle.

WOMAN: You did?

MAN: I tried to ask for what I wanted with respect.

WOMAN: Really?

MAN: Yes.

WOMAN: With respect.

MAN: Yes, but...

WOMAN: But...?

MAN: But that didn't work.

WOMAN: Why didn't it work?

MAN: The women never cooperated when I treated them with respect.

WOMAN: I see. But they cooperated when you were disrespectful?

Pause. MAN looks at the WOMAN.

WOMAN: Were you always the one questioning the women?

MAN: Yes.

WOMAN: Women are your specialty?

The WOMAN laughs.

MAN: Look, I'm sorry about what happened to you. But I was only doing what I was told.

WOMAN: Sure, you were. Only doing what you were told. What you've been taught. By every man you've known.... Right? How to get what you want from a woman?

MAN: I'm sorry that you were brought here. I'm sorry for whatever happened to you.

WOMAN: Thanks.

MAN: But killing me isn't the answer.

WOMAN: No?

Our choices about performers were based solely on logistics: who was able to travel that year; who was willing/ able to take on a particular role.

That said, *Chronicles from Kashmir* could be seen as a very heteronormative text. Would you agree or disagree with this statement? Why?

When we talk about change, in relation to social justice, what do we mean?

Are we speaking about a tangible, visible change in particular socio-economic or political conditions?

Or does change also refer to intangible shifts of consciousness?

Or, when we speak of change, do we mean shifts that lead to new mistakes, rather than a repetition of old ones?

Or, are we referring to change as choices that do less harm than others?

MAN: No.

WOMAN: So, what is the answer?

MAN: It depends on what you're looking for.

WOMAN: What if I don't know what I'm looking for?

MAN: Then doing this to me, killing me even, isn't going to change anything.

WOMAN: Maybe not. Maybe in the grand scheme of the world, or this war, it won't change anything. But for me, killing you can change everything.

MAN: But what if you make things worse?

WOMAN: Things can't get worse.

MAN: Things can always get worse.

WOMAN: Killing you... will change things. Better or worse, I don't care. But something needs to change.

MAN: You just want a change.

WOMAN: Yes.

MAN: Then you should do it. You should kill me. Just get it over with.

Pause.

WOMAN: You done with the ro*tis?*

MAN nods.

> What is the dramatic/
> literary potential of
> ending this scene as a
> frozen vignette? As an
> unknown?
>
> What impact might
> have been achieved by
> unfreezing this moment
> and ending the scene by
> having the WOMAN shoot
> the MAN?

WOMAN: Stand up.

MAN stands up.

WOMAN: Take off those clothes.

MAN takes off the women's clothes he has been wearing. When he is back in his male clothes, WOMAN stands in front of him. She lifts the gun up in front of him. They lock eyes. Freeze.

The tap still drips.

As the WOMAN and MAN stand in silence, staring at each other with a gun between them, the GUIDES hand out stone souvenirs for the audience to keep inside their bags. Here, the souvenirs are accompanied by text along the lines of Women & War *(Rana & Berry, 2015).*

Once everyone in the audience receives their stone souvenirs, they are guided to the next space through a path down which they have to walk while performing a task. Perhaps they all have to keep a ball in the air while they walk — dropping the ball would result in the whole group having to go back to the starting point and begin walking the path again. The GUIDES need to say nothing more or less than: "We need to keep the ball in the air while we walk. If we don't, we have to go back and start our walk again."

INSTALLATION A

The sections called INSTALLATIONS in this script are
envisioned as museums, of sorts. Museums that are
composed of different kinds of exhibits: **interactive
questions** that require audience members to add their
responses — with pre-existing exemplars already written
in, if needed; **gallery components** that invite the audience
to watch/listen/witness; **word cluster displays** that
serve as commentaries on particular politics of language
vis-à-vis Kashmir's conflicts; **reading sections** where
audiences can choose to engage with, or ignore, polyvocal
narratives about a chosen theme; **Buzzfeed booths** where
spectators might immerse themselves in popular Bollywood
(re)imaginations of Kashmir.[1]

> What are the different
> pedagogical strategies
> at play in the installation
> spaces?
>
> *Hint: look at pedagogical
> concepts surrounding
> effective teaching/learning
> practices, especially in
> relation to active learning/
> experiential education/
> project-based learning.*

Although audience members may intentionally be made
uncomfortable through design choices in other scenes, it is important that the installation spaces
are comfortable: there should be spaces for the audience to sit down; to relax. The installations
should be set up in spaces that have easy access to restrooms; where there are specifically chosen
drinks and snacks that are made available [suggestions for the drink/food menus are made at
the end of each installation section].

As the spectators wander through any installation space, the GUIDES individually (and
informally) hand each of them a stone souvenir to place in their bag. The description of each
souvenir is included at the end of the respective installation's script.

On the door of each installation space, the following instructions should be posted clearly:

---

1   The media company's name is used as wordplay: to refer to these booths' focus on popular, mainstream
     media.

    https://doi.org/10.11647/OBP.0223.08

INSTRUCTIONS FOR THIS SPACE

This is your space.

A space to think,
to reflect,
to add your own voices to this tapestry of experiences.

You can choose to take a break while you explore this space:
go to the restroom
grab a snack
watch the film.
Please ask one of the GUIDES for help in finding what you
need.

You can always request a timeout and choose to rest in our
"sanctuary space." Again, simply let a GUIDE know if this is
what you need.

We pride ourselves on our hospitality.

The "sanctuary space" is a quiet room that is designated for nothing else: *no scenes; no installations. It is where spectators, escorted by a crewmember on audience duty, are taken if they need a break from the experience.*

The exhibits below are described in no particular order — each one will, ultimately, have to be installed as best fits the chosen site.

Exhibit #1: Interactive Question

The instruction below is posted in one part of the space; the audience is provided with materials with which they can add their responses.

Write about a time you were a part of something that
you did not agree with.

Exhibit #2: Interactive Question

A large black board with the question below; the audience is encouraged to write on the board with pieces of chalk.

What is discipline?

Exhibit #3: Gallery

The poem below, by Lalita Pandit, is displayed:

Anantnag
(Pandit, 1996)

I took pride in your
natural springs,
your navigable river.
Every April we went
to Mattan, offered libations
to the dead: my father's dead
my mother's.
No dead of my own then,
life was eternal.
I could sense it when we
gathered blue lotuses
to lay at a gold-plated
doorstep, bronze sun disk:
majestic, bedazzling.

Thirty years journeyed
past us, leaving behind
hoof taps on stone.
Spring and autumn skies
grew old, listening
to night *ragas*.
Un-chronicled silences
of a very cold moon.

Apple trees you planted
in the backyard are tired
of bearing fruit.
They no longer blossom
in early spring;
their leaves look pensive,
yellowed at the edges.

Whoever opens the front gate
will close it fast in my face,
without asking my name.
Still, my expatriate feet drag me
back to you.

Evening shadows stare at me
with blind eyes. Cool breezes
say: may be, only may be,
we knew you then.
What of that? Now you are
a stranger, an enemy.

Piles of garbage along
the hospital walls, broken bottles,
blood soaked bandages.

Black curtains on windows
tell me to go where I came
from. Children stare with
suspicion. They have learnt
to hate; they are afraid.

Hollow eyed ghosts
walk the streets
beneath a thin moon, muttering
curses, adding up the dead.
The hill looks like a camel's back.
It is haunted.

Exhibit #4: Interactive Question

An open trunk with the instruction below; audience members write their answers on pieces of paper and place them inside the trunk.

> If you were forced to leave home — possibly forever — and could only take the things that you could carry yourself, what would you take?

Exhibit #5: Word Cluster

The following words are displayed — together, apart, on the floor, on the ceiling — whatever best fits the space.

> Displaced person
> Asylum seeker
> Refugee
> Migrant
> Exile
> Runaway
> Escapee
> Fugitive

Exhibit #6: Reading Gallery

Below are suggested readings that are made available in this installation space — articles about the Kashmiri Pandit exodus from different points of view. Audience members should be invited to peruse them, at their convenience.

Rahul Pandita's (2013) *On Kashmir and its Stories*

Ather Zia's (2008) *Q & A with Sanjay Kak*

Muntaha Hafizi's (2015) *Leaving Home*

T. N. Madan's (2015) *Old Memories and Recent Encounters from a Kashmir We Have Irretrievably Los*t

Nitasha Kaul's (2013) *The Idea of India and Kashmir*

Varad Sharma's (2017) *The Prolonged Wait: Kashmir Lives on in the Hearts and Minds of Pandits*

Varad Sharma's (2016) *A Pandit POV: Why the Discussion on Jammu and Kashmir is Half-Baked and Dishonest*

Any/all comments from *A Query for Rahul Pandita: Why Are You Ignoring the Existence of a Kashmiri Brotherhood?* (Scroll.in, 2016)

Kundan Lal Chowdhury's (2016) *Kashmiri Pandits Remember January 19, 1990: 'It is for your own good to leave'*

Any/all comments from *Readers' Comments: 'Kashmir belongs equally to Pandits who were driven out, Harsh Mander'* (Scroll.in, 2017)

Rahul Pandita's (2016) *The Ugly Truth Behind a ''Heartwarming' Story of Muslims Performing a Kashmiri Pandit's Last Rites*

Exhibit #7: Buzzfeed Booth

> How do you interpret the use of Bollywood in *Chronicles from Kashmir*?

A poster of the Bollywood film *Kashmir ki Kali* is pasted alongside a screening of the same film; the audio comes through speakers and in so doing, becomes the soundscape for the installation space. There is no escaping Bollywood depictions of Kashmir, is there?

There should be comfortable seating spaces in front of the screening, allowing spectators to rest and simply watch the video, should they desire to do so.

Suggested Menu for this Installation Space

A snack, and a drink, that are particular to the Kashmiri Pandit community. For ideas, see Amit Hirmath's (2013) *The Gastronomical Affair of a Kashmiri Pandit Wedding* and Shivangana Vasudeva's (2017) *Beyond Wazwan: A Peek into the Cuisine of Kashmiri Pandits.*

> *Wazwaan*
> A multi-course meal that is particular to Kashmir, served during celebratory occasions

Stone Souvenir

During the installation, just as in the preceding scenes, the GUIDES give spectators a souvenir to carry in their bags. Here, the souvenir is a stone that has wrapped around it a piece of paper containing extracts from a text like *Kashmir's Exile Poetry: An Aesthetic of Loss* (Shameem, 2016).

After the spectators have had about 30 minutes to explore the installation space, the GUIDES invite the audience to exit.

As the audience exits this space and moves on to the next one, they walk along a path that is designed using a variety of suitcases, trunks, bags: objects that are associated with migration.

Scene Four: The Artists

▶ WATCH THE VIDEO

The GUIDES knock on a door.

GUIDE #2: Can we come in, Director? I've brought the people I was telling you about.

DIRECTOR: Yes, yes. Please come in everyone. Take a seat and enjoy our rehearsal!

Three ACTORS (ACTOR #1, ACTRESS, ACTOR #2) and a DIRECTOR are in the middle of a rehearsal. The DIRECTOR is yelling out directions to the actors and they respond accordingly.

The scene being rehearsed is as follows: A young Kashmiri woman (ACTRESS) is in love with a man (ACTOR #1) that her family doesn't approve of. Her disapproving brother (ACTOR #2) is now trying to get her married to someone else. The scene is scripted to represent a fight between the brother and the lover, with the young woman stuck between them. The scene being rehearsed is set to culminate with the entry of a POLICEMAN who has been called by the neighbours to stop the fight.

There are various critiques that the ACTORS and DIRECTOR receive in this scene.

From these critiques, if you had to make educated guesses about the challenges that Kashmiri artists face, what would they be?

For the sake of clarity, the police character that exists in the scene being rehearsed by the ACTORS and DIRECTOR is hereon referred to as the SCRIPTED POLICEMAN. The other police character is referred to as the UNSCRIPTED POLICEMAN.

When the audience enters, the DIRECTOR is staging the fight and the ACTORS are following his directions. After a minute or two to establish the nature of the scene for the audience, the UNSCRIPTED POLICEMAN enters.

 https://doi.org/10.11647/OBP.0223.09

UNSCRIPTED
POLICEMAN: What's happening here?

DIRECTOR: Who are you? Our policeman's casting has been done. Please leave. If you
    want another role, please wait outside. Our show has been cast.

*The DIRECTOR and ACTORS #1 & #2 push the UNSCRIPTED POLICEMAN toward the
door and heads back to the rehearsal.*

DIRECTOR: I don't know where these crappy actors come from. Let's continue.

*The ACTORS go back to the positions they were in before the UNSCRIPTED POLICEMAN
entered. Rehearsal proceeds.*

UNSCRIPTED
POLICEMAN: Stop. You have to listen to me.

DIRECTOR: Sir, I already told you that --

UNSCRIPTED
POLICEMAN: Quiet. I know you are making a plan to poison her.

DIRECTOR: What?

UNSCRIPTED
POLICEMAN: You're trying to kill her. Look, I have proof.

UNSCRIPTED POLICEMAN produces a bottle.

DIRECTOR: What?

UNSCRIPTED
POLICEMAN: We know everything.

DIRECTOR goes to look at the bottle.

ACTRESS: Have they added this to the script?

ACTOR #1: Who knows. This director keeps changing the scene every day. Come on,
    let's improvise with them.

Both ACTORS walk toward the UNSCRIPTED POLICEMAN.

ACTOR #2: I'm her brother and I can decide whether to give her death, or life.

ACTOR #1: I can decide too, because I love her.

ACTRESS: Please sir, stop this fight.

The SCRIPTED POLICEMAN enters.

SCRIPTED
POLICEMAN: QUIET. QUIET. QUIET. QUIE- Wait. Who is this guy?

DIRECTOR: Look, this is our play's policeman. Who are you?

UNSCRIPTED
POLICEMAN: I've come from the police station.

Silence. All actors exit with the UNSCRIPTED POLICEMAN. A few seconds of silence.

GUIDE #1: Is that it?

GUIDE #2: I'm not sure, actually. This didn't happen the last time I was here.

GUIDE #1: Should we go see where they are?

GUIDE #2: I'm sure they are — look, there they are.

The DIRECTOR and ACTORS come back into the room. SCRIPTED POLICEMAN is hereon referred to as ACTOR #3.

GUIDE #1: Aha, Director *saab*. Did you sort out the confusion?

The DIRECTOR looks at the GUIDES. He doesn't say anything. He walks back to his chair. The ACTORS take their positions again.

DIRECTOR: Let's try something else this time, ok? I don't want to go back to the old play. Let's do something traditional, instead. That will lighten all our spirits.

The actors perform a rouf *dance: a dance that is said to be used in — sometimes problematic — cultural "showcases" of Kashmir's traditions. While it is near impossible to script, in written form, the choreography for this, it is recommended that producers of* Chronicles from Kashmir *reach out to Kashmiris in their vicinity to explore whether they might learn elements of the form.*

> *Rouf*
> A folk-dance form
> performed by women in
> Kashmir

The actor playing the UNSCRIPTED POLICEMAN re-enters as an ART CRITIC towards the very end of the dance.

ART CRITIC: What is this you're doing here?

DIRECTOR: Sir, we are just trying our hand at some traditional Kashmiri performance.

ART CRITIC: Please, keep going.

The actors sing and dance some more. When they are done, the ART CRITIC begins to clap.

ART CRITIC: You are all very talented. This is wonderful work! You know what, I really want to find a way to get more people to see your piece.

DIRECTOR: Really? Thank you so much, sir.

ART CRITIC: Yes, yes. We'll go to festivals across the world and we will show them how beautiful and ancient Kashmiri culture is.

DIRECTOR: Thank you so much, sir. That would be wonderful.

ART CRITIC: We can sell tickets and of course, all of you will be paid. Let me see a little bit more of this wonderful performance — I love what I have seen so far!

DIRECTOR: Actors, why don't we show him that speech. You know, the one about the pigeons?

> *Bhand Pather*
> Traditional folk theatre of Kashmir

Look into the form of *Bhand Pather*. Consider its history, evolution, and potential.

In keeping with the satirical approach of *Bhand Pather*, ACTOR #3's monologue about "pigeons" functions as socio-political commentary.

What is it commenting on?

What is the subtext?

The ACTORS mutter their agreement and set up. ACTOR #3 stands on the backs of ACTORS #1 & #2 and performs the following speech in an extremely loud volume (a piece that alludes to stylistic elements from Bhand Pather*).*

ACTOR #3: Attention, attention.

People of this village please listen to me.

Pigeons from here have flown there and have been caged.

Pigeons from there have flown here and have been caged.

Our horses have been afflicted with an unknown disease...

Maybe from eating the grass there;

Maybe from eating the hay here;

Or maybe everything, here and there, has become infected?

In any case, the only certainty is that death looms large.

Here.

And There.

The DIRECTOR and the ACTRESS are laughing during the entire speech and clap loudly when it is over. The ART CRITIC, however, is quiet.

ART CRITIC: I see...

DIRECTOR: What do you think, sir?

ART CRITIC: Yes. Yes. This has potential but... look, we will have to be careful. You need to edit the piece so that all this kind of obvious political commentary is taken out and we are only focusing on the beauty of Kashmiri culture.

DIRECTOR: But sir, as you know, political satire is an important part of *Bhand Pather*. It's integral to the piece, don't you think? Without it, the performance would not be true to the original form.

ART CRITIC: Look Director *saab*, we need to sell this piece and in order to get the kind of funding we need to take this piece outside Kashmir, we will have to be careful about what we say.

DIRECTOR: Sell it? But sir, this is art, don't you think —

ART CRITIC: Look, young man. Don't you want to make some money from your work? Don't you want your actors to make a living?

DIRECTOR: Of course, sir, but —

ART CRITIC: Look Mr. Director, you need to be willing to be a bit flexible about these things. If you are not ready to do this, someone else will be.

DIRECTOR: Ok, sir. Let's try your suggestions.

The ACTORS set up the same image. This time, the ART CRITIC interrupts ACTOR #3 after the first few limes of the speech and instructs ACTOR #3 to step down from the backs of ACTORS #1 & #2 while speaking. The ACTORS look at the DIRECTOR for permission to do this — which the DIRECTOR grudgingly gives.

When ACTOR #3 speaks from his new position, again, the ART CRITIC interrupts his speech and asks ACTOR #3 to speak at a lower volume. The ACTOR once again looks at the DIRECTOR for permission to do this— which the DIRECTOR, even more grudgingly, gives.

When ACTOR #3 starts the speech the third time — with the new position and volume — the ART CRITIC starts to instruct him to change the text that refers to "one side" and the "other side."

ART CRITIC: Don't say "this side" and "the other side." Instead —

Incensed, the DIRECTOR interrupts.

DIRECTOR: PLEASE STOP THIS.

Silence.

ART CRITIC: Excuse me?

DIRECTOR: I'm sorry, sir, but you're changing the whole piece. You're taking away the essence of the performance.

ART CRITIC: The essence of the... (*He laughs*). You have no idea how the market works do you, son? You think people are going to pay money to come and see you criticize the government? You think people are going to pay money to hear your political ideas? No. People will come to see the Kashmiri music, costumes, and culture.

DIRECTOR: Politics are part of our culture, sir. You cannot expect to create effective art, relevant art, with no politics involved!

ART CRITIC: That is exactly what I expect. No politics. Look, as I said before, if you are not willing to do this, I'll find another group of artists that will be more amenable to creating what I'm looking for. You have two days — let me know what you decide.

The ART CRITIC exits. The ACTORS and DIRECTOR look at each other.

> *Bhand Pather*
> Traditional folk theatre of
> Kashmir

DIRECTOR: Look. This is not working. Let's try something else for now. Let's move away from the *Bhand Pather* and try something more experimental and movement-based. Maybe that way, if we are more abstract in the way that we are political, people will not be averse to our work?

The ACTORS begin to do a movement-based piece. Instrumental music plays. The ACTORS perform a choreography that uses tools from contemporary dance to showcase a protest between civilians pelting stones, and the police/armed forces.

The actor playing the UNSCRIPTED POLICEMAN and ART CRITIC re-enters during the piece as a fellow ARTIST. A friend of the DIRECTOR, the ARTIST is greeted with air of warmth and joviality. When the movement-based piece ends:

ARTIST: Hmm ... what is this you have here?

DIRECTOR: Sir, it's a movement-based piece that comments on the state of affairs in Kashmir. It's an experimental piece that uses physicality to depict issues like torture and...

ARTIST: Please, let me just stop you right there. I don't understand why you young artists keep doing all this experimental nonsense. Aren't you forgetting all our local traditions and culture with work like this?

DIRECTOR: Sir, we're just trying something new. Just because we're doing some experimental work it doesn't mean that we're forgetting our traditions and —

ARTIST: Stop trying these new things and just tell the truth. The scene that you have showed here does not do any justice to the reality of what's happening in Kashmir. You think this movement captures the reality of what we have lived? Of what we are living? Let me tell you something. With this kind of piece, it's like you are showing a field. You are painting the picture of a large field, but you are not paying attention to the plants and the animals and the farmers without whom that field wouldn't be a field.

DIRECTOR: I don't understand what you're saying, sir —

ARTIST: You are not being honest, Director *saab*. You are showing a general idea of pain; a general idea of suffering. You are not naming the names of the people who all of us know are implicated in the pain and the suffering. Why don't you name the names!

DIRECTOR: Sir, this is just one performance. We can't show everything in one performance. We have to —

ARTIST: I expected better from you. You have sold out just like everyone else.

DIRECTOR: Sir, I —

ARTIST: You have sold out just like everyone else.

The ARTIST walks out of the room in a huff. Long silence.

ACTOR #1: Sir, what do we do now?

DIRECTOR: I don't know.

Silence.

ACTRESS: Sir, can I say something?

DIRECTOR: Yes?

ACTRESS: Why don't we just make theatre for ourselves?

DIRECTOR: What?

ACTRESS: Look, we are artists. We need to make theatre to... to be alive. Can't we just make theatre and not worry about what the authorities, and the critics, and other artists say about what we are doing?

ACTOR #2: Because then it's not theatre! Theatre needs an audience.

ACTRESS: I know theatre needs an audience, sir. But if everything we do is going to be criticized; if everything we do is going to be manipulated by someone, what's the point? We should either try to find new audiences or make this work for ourselves.

DIRECTOR: The point is that we are artists. What else are we supposed to do?

ACTRESS: Exactly, sir. We are artists. So, let's just make our art and stop caring so much about what other people say.

ACTOR #2: That's easy for you to say.

ACTRESS: Excuse me?

ACTOR #2: Look, I don't mean any offence, but your family is rich; you can afford to make art just for the sake of making art. But some of us have to make a living. We have families to feed; clothes to buy; school fees to pay. How can we do that if we're just making theatre for ourselves? How can we do that if we don't have financial support? How can we do that if we stay away from the authorities, and the critics, and our fellow artists? We need money too, don't we? Making art for ourselves sounds very romantic and idealistic but how will we put food in our stomachs? How will we survive?

ACTRESS: So, what do you suggest we do?

ACTOR #2: I don't know.

Silence.

DIRECTOR: Look. I think we need to take a break. I think we need to figure out how to move forward with this. I need some time to think.

The DIRECTOR exits. Awkward silence.

GUIDE #2: (*to GUIDE #1*) Should we go, *janab*?

> *Beta*
> Son (colloquially used as the equivalent of "my dear")

ACTOR #3: Sir, please. We can't let our guests leave like this. What will they think of us? We should try to lighten the mood a little.

GUIDE #1: It's fine, *beta*. These things happen and they need —

ACTRESS: Sir, sorry to interrupt but I have an idea — can I share it with you all?

GUIDE #2: Sure.

ACTRESS: (*to the audience*) You're all outsiders, right? Can one of you teach us a dance or song or something that is from where you are? We've never been outside Kashmir and we would love to learn something new.

GUIDE #2: That's a great idea — I'm sure some of us would like to learn something new too! Anyone here want to teach us something?

Audience members are given the opportunity, encouraged by the GUIDES, to teach the collective — i.e., the ACTORS and the spectator group — a performance-based "item" of their choice. If no spectator volunteers to do this, GUIDE #2 steps forward and teaches the group something.

After the teaching/learning process has continued for about 10 minutes and there is a sense of community in the air, the GUIDES walk around handing stone souvenirs to audience members and preparing them for their journey to the next space. Here, the stone souvenir is decorated with text along the lines of Artists in Times of War (Zinn, 2004).

When all the spectators have received their souvenirs, they are asked to bid farewell to the ACTORS and make their way to the next space. The path they walk along, this time, is a maze made of paper, canvas, paints, and pencils — the GUIDES and the audience can stop to add aesthetic elements to their path while they walk.

Scene Five: The Puppets

A POLICE OFFICER (PO) and an ARMED FORCES OFFICER (AO) stand in the middle of the room, facing each other. They wear masks. There are strings tied to their arms and legs. Maybe they are puppets?

Along the sides of the room, there are more actors who look like puppets. They too wear masks, and there are strings tied to their hands and feet that are then tethered to the ceiling; to the walls. Some of the actor-puppets might be dressed in police/army uniforms/as rebels. Others are dressed as civilians. As politicians. As particular media personalities. The strings from these puppets are also connected to AO and PO's strings. Every performer in the room is enmeshed within a complex, seemingly connected, web of strings that has no identifiable source.

When the spectators are all seated, we hear the sound of heartbeats. Mechanical. Automated.

> The chorus of puppets in the background have specifically chosen costume elements.
>
> If you had to interpret these choices for the chorus, in relation to your interpretation of the AO, PO, and LEADER characters, what would you say about their presence, effect, and their embodied subtext about the conflicts in Kashmir?

AO and PO do the mirror exercise where both performers coordinate movements while only looking in each other's eyes. For a time, the AO and PO's movements are effectively coordinated, and it is impossible to see which puppet is leading the other. Suddenly though, their movements become jerky and uncoordinated. We don't know who is making the mistake, the PO or the AO.

AO and PO try, a few more times, with unsuccessful results. Every time they fail, the sound of the heartbeats stops — only to restart a few seconds later, when they make a fresh attempt. With every failure to coordinate, however, AO and PO's frustration builds.

They keep trying till LEADER enters.

AO & PO: Good morning, sir.

LEADER: How is it coming along?

AO: We're having some trouble sir. It starts off well and then... then it all collapses.

   https://doi.org/10.11647/OBP.0223.10

LEADER: Show me.

AO and PO try the mirror exercise again and fail again.

LEADER: Let's try this.

LEADER stands behind AO and guides his hands. This time, the synchronization works perfectly.

LEADER: See? It works.

AO: With your help it works, sir, but...

PO: But how can we do it without you?

LEADER: You'll never have to. Don't you know that?

AO and PO freeze. The LEADER looks at the audience.

> How do you interpret the choice to include the AO and PO as two different entities, rather than as one character of "government employees"?
>
> Who, or what, does the LEADER represent?

LEADER: With my command, anyone can do this —let's try with those two (*pointing at the GUIDES*).

LEADER gives the GUIDES similar masks to those worn by the AO, PO, and actor puppets. LEADER stands behind GUIDE #1 and tries to make sure that both GUIDES synchronize their actions. However, this time, the LEADER's efforts don't work so well, and the two GUIDES are unable to synchronize.

Throughout the GUIDES' attempts and all those that follow — until mentioned otherwise— the sound of the mechanical heartbeat stops every time the mirror-exercise partners fail to coordinate, restarting when new attempts are made, and continuing only if/when coordination succeeds.

Each pair of mirror-exercise partners is given masks before they try the activity. If the pair succeeds, they get to keep their masks. If they fail, the LEADER takes their masks back.

So, when the GUIDES fail to coordinate, the LEADER takes their masks away and the sound stops:

LEADER: Something is wrong with these two. Let me try with someone else. Who would like to try this? I can pay you if you want...

Two ACTORS in AUDIENCE volunteer immediately. The LEADER gives them masks, the sound starts, and the LEADER does the exercise with them. It works!

LEADER: See, it works as long as you are willing to accept my help.

The two ACTORS in AUDIENCE join the other two background actor/puppets.

LEADER: Anyone else?

Audience members are given a chance to volunteer. The LEADER performs the exercise with them. If they succeed, they join the two ACTORS in AUDIENCE within the puppet image (the LEADER shows them how). If the audience members cannot manage to coordinate, they do not get to join the image. In this case, like the GUIDES, they are told that something is wrong with them. The LEADER continues this activity as long as there are volunteers from the audience.

Once there are no more volunteers, the recording of the heartbeat gets louder and begins to morph. The heartbeat, at the beginning, still sounds extremely artificial. However, the sound changes almost imperceptibly, and becomes more 'human' by the end of the sequence described below.

In this sequence, the LEADER 'activates' the puppets individually, by touching them on the head. As soon as they are activated, the actors begin to move in jerky movements. The puppet-audience members are activated too, and they can choose to follow what the actors are doing.

> How do you interpret the symbolism of the mirror exercise?

Or not. Eventually, one of the puppets starts to jerk free from the ropes that tie him to the ceiling. His strings start to break. The puppet is breaking free.

AO and PO begin efforts to control him. The actor-puppet resists. In response to his resistance, some of the other puppets start to act more aggressively too, as if they are trying to break out of their strings. The AO and PO eventually manage to hold down the resisting puppet and 'deactivate' him by touching him on the head in the same way that the LEADER activated him.

As soon as this actor has been suppressed, all the other puppets go back to behaving as they were before the resistance: simply making jerky movements. There is no more resistance. AO and PO also return to their own movements. Unbeknownst to everyone, the LEADER has quietly left the room during the actor-puppet's resistance. No one knows/should notice when he disappears.

The sounds stop. Silence.

GUIDE #1 slowly get up, takes out a pair of scissors and cuts the strings holding each puppet. As he does, he asks each one "What if they did not control you?" *Each time he is met with silence and a blank stare before the puppet walks out of the room.*

GUIDE #1 cuts the puppet-spectators' strings as well, asks them the same question, and directs them back to their seats.

> If you could complete the puppet's last line "Then, maybe..." what would you say?

Finally, GUIDE #1 reaches the last puppet, the one who resisted. When the actor asks this puppet "What if they did not control you?" *the puppet looks back at him and replies,* "Then maybe…"

The last puppet smiles, and in a bizarre image covered in string, this actor hands out stone souvenirs to the audience while the GUIDES watch him with curiosity: these souvenirs are wrapped with a paper that has pictorial instructions for how to build a puppet drawn on it.

The GUIDES invite the audience to follow them to the next space by walking down a path that is evocatively designed with puppets.

INSTALLATION B

The general instructions that introduce INSTALLATION A also apply here. The exhibits below are described in no particular order — each one will, ultimately, have to be installed as best fits the chosen site.

Exhibit #1: Interactive question

The prompt below is hung on a large piece of canvas or an easel, with the materials needed for audience members to paint their responses:

> Paint. Your. Pain.

Like many aspects in this script, the "Gallery" and "Interactive question" sections of the installations are ones that are meant to be adapted to fit the time and place in which the work is being staged.

So, if you were to stage this work in your context — wherever that may be — how would you evolve the ideas that are included in this installation?

Exhibit #2: Gallery

Art by Kashmiri artists adorns this space: works are displayed on the walls; on the floors; on the ceiling — a testament to the creativity that thrives in the region. Consider the following:

https://doi.org/10.11647/OBP.0223.11

Paintings by Masood Hussain (Saatchi Art, 2018)

Wasim Mushtaq Wani's (2013) curation in *Art of Protest in Kashmir*

Majid Maqbool's (2016) showcasing of cartoonists

Malik Sajad's (2015) graphic novel

Sanjay Kak's (2011) Until My Freedom Has Come

Poems from Suvir Kaul's (2015) *Of Gardens and Graves: Essays on Kashmir | Poems in Translation*

Exhibit #3: Interactive Question

Audience members are invited to add their responses to the following question:

What are you willing to fight for, and how?

Exhibit #4: Word Cluster

The following words are displayed, in whatever fashion best fits the space:

Terrorist
Militant
Commander
Hero
Rebel
Revolutionary
Martyr
Freedom Fighter

Exhibit #5: Activity

Audience members are provided with the materials they might need to engage with the following instructions. The spectators' designs must then be displayed, becoming part of the installation for future audiences:[1]

How would you articulate the goals of Exhibit #5 in this installation, especially in relation to the following scene?

Design a jail for 3,011 inmates	Design a jail for 2,406 inmates	Design a jail for 920 inmates
Design a jail for 450 inmates	Design a jail for 60 inmates	Design a jail for 15,000 inmates

Exhibit #6: Simulation

A recreated prison cell, one that is reflective of current conditions in such facilities in Kashmir. For context, see Basant Rath's (2017) *Why We Need to Talk About the Condition of India's Prisons*. A sign is posted outside the construction, inviting audiences to enter the constructed cell.

What are the ethical questions to consider when designing/implementing a simulation like Exhibit #6?

What are some steps to take in addressing the ethical questions that you've identified?

Exhibit #7: Buzzfeed Booth

The poster for the Bollywood movie *Fanaa* is pasted alongside a screening of the film; the audio comes through speakers and in so doing, becomes the soundscape for the installation space. There should be comfortable seating spaces in front of the screening, allowing spectators to rest and simply watch the video, should they desire to do so.

---

1 The numbers included in the instructions are from a 2015 disclosure of prison populations in Jammu & Kashmir (*Times of India*, 2015).

Suggested Menu for this Installation Space

Slightly watered-down tea, with snacks that are ordered from a place like the Tihar Jail Initiative's Bakery (Tihar Jail Initiative, 2017).

Stone Souvenir

During the installation, just as in the preceding scenes, the GUIDES give spectators a stone souvenir to carry in their bags. Here, the stone is covered with images like those created by Banksy (see Moloney, 2017).

An informal conversation occurs between the GUIDES while the audience meanders through the installation.

> *Janab*
> Your Excellency
> (a colloquialism that is
> used to connote respect,
> regardless of the gender
> of the person being
> addressed)

GUIDE #1: It's a complex situation isn't it, *janab*? The struggle of the artist in Kashmir...

GUIDE #2: I think that the struggles that artists face here are not limited to Kashmir. These are struggles that are being faced by artists across the world. How does one make a living through the arts?

How does one balance the richness of tradition with the joys that come with experimentation? Where is the line between making art that sells and selling one's voice as an artist? These are important questions that artists have faced, still face, and will continue to face, across time and space.

GUIDE #1: But isn't there something about a place like Kashmir that makes the struggles different?

GUIDE #2: What do you mean?

GUIDE #1: Well, I've never met artists from outside Kashmir so I can't be sure. But it seems to me that artists here, they have to have a fire; a burning inside them to commit to their art in the face of violence and family obligation and censorship and fear. They need to find a way for their unique Kashmiri identities to come out through their work... that isn't easy.

GUIDE #2: I don't imagine that it's easy at all. Being caught between all these struggles can be exhausting, I'm sure. Do you see any particular solutions that might address what these actors are facing though?

GUIDE #1: I don't have any solutions but seeing this group's experience has made me want to think about it more... In one sense, it begins with our children, doesn't it? When we tell them that they should become doctors and engineers and lawyers, but very rarely do we tell them to become artists. So, it starts there, and because we've created a culture where the arts are not valued as much as other things here — when the people who do want to become artists go out into the world, they are faced with nothing but challenges. Add to that the fear of censorship... where artists become afraid to say what they're thinking because of fear of repercussions not only from expected sources like the government and other armed agencies, but also from the harsh criticism from their peers and neighbours and families... I honestly don't know how some of Kashmir's artists have found the strength to keep going.

GUIDE #2: I must say though that despite all these challenges, I have been amazed by the number of creative and artistic people I have met in Kashmir. There seems to be a growing spirit of entrepreneurship and creativity here; people who are writing poems and articles and movies and songs and plays... It's admirable. I don't know where they find the fight...

The conversation continues informally, and improvised; or it just winds down.

After 30 minutes, the GUIDES ask the audience to follow them to the next location.

As the audience exits this space and moves on to the next one, they walk along a path that is designed using thick ropes.

Scene Six: The Incarcerated

WATCH THE VIDEO

They reach the doorway of another room. A prison. The LADY is already present.

During the monologue each of the following monologues, the LADY is staged at a location in the middle of the space. Through directorial choices, it is signified that she symbolically takes on the role of each person that a particular PRISONER is speaking about. The stage directions below each PRISONER's text describe the LADY's actions.

PRISONER 1: By becoming a rebel, one can lose everything. My wife has left me, married someone else, taken my things, my child... The rebel movement... I joined because it was the thing to do at the time. There didn't seem to be any other choice. Some of us became rebels for the money, some of us did it for fun, some did it because they were unemployed, and they thought it better to die for a cause rather than dying a little bit every day from hunger

> The PRISONERS have been intentionally described in ambiguous terms.
>
> Who do you think they represent?
>
> Why the ambiguity?

While the monologue is spoken by PRISONER 1, LADY takes on the role of his child. The child speaks two lines: "When I grow up, I want to be like my father" and "When I grow up, I do not want to be like my father" As the child says these lines, she is playing with her toys. She murmurs the lines quietly. She continues her murmurs even when PRISONER #1 has finished speaking. Her muttering pierces the silence. PRISONER 1 watches her. A few seconds.

Freeze.

The first song.

PRISONER 2: What about those of us who actually believed in the struggle? Who will not break for anything? I became a rebel for the freedom of my nation. Becoming a

https://doi.org/10.11647/OBP.0223.12

rebel is a noble undertaking...When justice is gone, what room is there for peace? I... I spit on profit. I spit on people who joined because they thought it would be romantic to be a hero. I spit on those who used the movement for their own gain. I spit on them. I SPIT ON THEM. I SPIT ON THEM. Thoo. Thoo. Thoo. Thoo. Thoo.

the monologue spoken by PRISONER 2, the LADY takes on the role of his mother. This mother has become a beggar after her son was taken to prison. She expected that maybe her son's rebel colleagues would take care of her — her son was a hero after all. But she hasn't been provided with anything. She begs for money, unsure what else to do to make ends meet, but it is important that she is proud of what her son did. She walks around amidst the audience. She says one line "My son was a hero. Help me in his name." *LADY continues her murmurs even when PRISONER #2 has finished speaking. Her mumbled begging pierces the silence. PRISONER #2 watches her. A few seconds.*

Freeze.

The second song.

PRISONER #3: My wife married me while her parents would have never tolerated a man like me on their doorstep. When we were first together, we shared one blanket. If I moved, she was out of it, if she moved, I was out of it. What could I give her? All our women who have come from across the border, there needs to be support for them to go back home. They need to be able to see their families again.... But instead, what they face here... People say to me: "Who have you brought home? Couldn't you have brought a Kashmiri?"

While the monologue of PRISONER #3 is being spoken, the LADY becomes a wife who has now turned to prostitution to make ends meet. Unable to see her husband, unable to ask for support from her parents or in-laws, she has no option but to... you know. The way she shows this is subtle — a change in clothes, an adding-on of make-up; cultural codes that show she has had to step out. PRISONER #3 watches her. A few seconds.

In this text, the LADY's character is portrayed by one performer rather than multiple performers.

What might be the impact of this choice, as compared to that of casting different performers in each of the LADY's characters?

Freeze.

The third song.

PRISONER #4: I am NOT a rebel. I am innocent. I am not a rebel. I am innocent. I AM NOT A REBEL. I AM INNO-

While PRISONER #4 speaks, the woman wipes off her make-up and goes back to being a neutral LADY.

The PRISONERS begin to sing the fourth song collectively; one that might be coming from the LADY's inner world. We don't know who is singing; it doesn't matter.

As the PRISONERS sing, the LADY walks from prisoner to prisoner with increasing speed — as herself; as the mother; as the child; as the wife — till she's finally running. Sprinting. And ultimately, collapsing on the ground.

Freeze.

GUIDE #1: So, these are the stories of rebellion that you've heard in Kashmir?

GUIDE #2: Yes, that's right.

GUIDE #1: You do know that there are different kinds of rebels in Kashmir, right? Not just the ones who might be called 'militants'?

GUIDE #2: Of course, sir; I realize that. But it has been hard to find those voices that will readily admit to why and how they are rebels... I can understand that, since there will be risks to sharing that with an outsider like me... Tell me, *janab*, who are some of the rebels you think I should speak to?

GUIDE #1: Why don't we ask our guests here what they think? I can always tell you my thoughts later, but I think this would be a wonderful opportunity for you to hear more opinions.

GUIDE #1 turns to the audience and tries to evoke responses — who do they think are rebels? Who are the rebellious voices that an outsider to Kashmir needs to hear? GUIDE #1 structures this like a conversation that would take place in a classroom/lecture and calls out the names of audience members from their badges. During this discussion GUIDE #2 hands stone souvenirs to each audience member. The stones are covered with a letter from a prisoner of war, from anywhere.

When the discussion has reached a natural pause: the first song.

For a moment, imagine that you do not have to stick to Kashmiri songs in the indicated sections but rather, can make any musical/sound choice that captures the shifting sentiments of this scene.

What would your musical score be?

PRISONER #1 walks out from his jail cell. LADY sits up and takes on the role of the child again. PRISONER #1 walks over to the child, sits down in front of her. They look at each other for a few seconds, in silence.

LADY
(as child): You're back.

PRISONER #1: I'm back.

Silence.

LADY

(as child): I'm sorry, papa. But I don't know how to talk to you.

PRISONER #1: We'll learn how to talk to each other. We have all the time in the world now.

LADY

(as child): You're not going to go away again?

PRISONER #1: I'm not going to go away again. I promise... You know, it was only the thought of seeing you that kept me going. Without the thought of you; without knowing that I would have you to come home to; I don't know if I would have made it out of prison.

LADY

(as child): It was that bad?

PRISONER #1: It was worse than anything you could have imagined... But that's all behind us now. Now, the only thing I have to worry about is how I can give you everything you want.

LADY

(as child): Why were you in jail for, papa?

PRISONER #1: What did your mother tell you?

LADY

(as child): Nothing.

Pause.

LADY

(as child): Have they forgiven you now?

PRISONER #1: No; no, they haven't.

LADY

(as child): So, how come they let you out?

PRISONER #1: Because some people decided it was time...

LADY

(as child): Even though you weren't forgiven?

PRISONER #1: Even though I wasn't forgiven.

LADY

(as child): Have you forgiven yourself, papa?

PRISONER #1: What?

LADY
(as child): Have you forgiven yourself?

The smile slowly fades from PRISONER 1's face. Freeze.

The second song.

PRISONER #2 walks out from his jail cell. LADY takes on the role of the mother. PRISONER #2 walks over to his mother, sits down in front of her. They look at each other for a few seconds, in silence.

LADY
(as mother): You're back.

PRISONER #2: I'm back, ma.

LADY
(as mother): You have no idea how much I have missed you.

PRISONER #2: Can't be more than I missed you.

LADY
(as mother): Look at you. You've gotten so skinny.

PRISONER #2 smiles.

LADY
(as mother): What now?

PRISONER #2: You know what I have to do, ma.

LADY
(as mother): You're going to join them again?

PRISONER #2: I have to. I have to fight.

LADY
(as mother): Why does it have to be you? Can't someone else do the fighting?

PRISONER #2: If everyone thought that way, nothing would change.

LADY
(as mother): But *beta*, what has changed with your fighting? All that has changed is that I have had to... I have had to beg. That's all that changed.

PRISONER #2 freezes in position.

The third song.

PRISONER #3 walks out from his jail cell. As he is doing so, LADY takes on the role of his wife and starts putting on make-up. PRISONER #3 walks over to his wife, sits down in front of her. They look at each other for a few seconds, in silence.

LADY
(as wife): You're back.

PRISONER #3: I'm back.

PRISONER #3 watches her put on the make-up. After a few moments of silence, he takes the make-up out of her hands, takes a handkerchief out of his pocket, and wipes the make-up slowly and deliberately off her face. As he does this, tears roll down her face. Once he has taken off all her make-up —

PRISONER #3: You don't have to do this anymore.

LADY
(as wife): Have you found a job?

Silence. They look at each other. He picks up the handkerchief again and takes it to her face. He wipes the make-up off. She tries to put it back on. A struggle. He knocks the make up out of her hands and they fall to the floor. PRISONER #3 freezes.

LADY becomes her original character: not the child, the mother, or the wife. She sings the fourth song that the PRISONERS were singing earlier. As she sings, she slowly walks out of the room.

PRISONER #4 walks out from his jail cell and walks to PRISONERS #1, #2 & #3, shaking them and bringing them out of their frozen positions while repeating the lines "I'm innocent. I didn't do anything." The three previously frozen actors get more and more agitated by PRISONER #4, until:

PRISONERS
#1, #2, #3: SHUT UP.

Silence.

GUIDE #2: Shall we?

GUIDE #1: Please, lead the way.

As the audience members are led out of this space and to the next one, they walk down a path of smoke and ashes...

Scene Seven: The Soldiers

[QR code] ▶ WATCH THE VIDEO

They reach the next space.

The room contains an installation of women's clothes, of various ages. Women's clothes are nailed to the ceiling; others are strewn on the floor. It is important that the installation is as vague as it is direct; as abstract as it is realistic.

> How do you interpret the presence and use of women's clothes in this scene?

When the audience walks in, they see four soldiers who are just hanging around (SOLDIER #1, SOLDIER #2, SOLDIER #3, SOLDIER #4).

SOLDIER #4: Ah, there you are...

GUIDE #2: Hello again, sir. Please take your seats everyone. I've asked these soldiers to talk to you about something, or someone, that they are waiting for in their lives. So please, take your seats and let's hear what they have to say to us!

SOLDIER #4 nods at SOLDIER #1, who walks through/around the crowd in an intimidating fashion.

SOLDIER #1: You want to hear my story? Stand in three straight lines. Close your eyes. Raise your hands above your head. (*During the course of the following monologue, SOLDIER #1 interrupts his story, correcting audience members' positions should they be faltering in their stances*). What am I waiting for? Hmm.... you know, two years ago I was living in Jammu. It was raining heavily and I was thinking of the assignment I had to complete and submit the next day. Amidst all this, I heard the melodious sound of a flute coming from somewhere. I turned my head around to find an old man sitting on the doorstep of an old people's home, playing the flute in the most incredible way I had ever heard. Tears were rolling down his cheeks.... This man sat on the doorstep every day, playing his flute, waiting, hoping that his son — his son who had just left him there — would realize his mistake and come back for him.

https://doi.org/10.11647/OBP.0223.13

It's just...fathers and sons just have this bond, you know? My father was an army man and when I got into the Academy, he was happier than I was. Seeing his joy, his pride, seeing that I might be able to do for him what the flute-playing man's son does not.... I am waiting for the day my father will see me in this uniform, with stars shining in his eyes, flagging off the aircraft which is being flown by his son.

SOLDIER #2: ABOUT TURN. Stand at ease. Attention. Squat and hold your arms out in front of you. DO IT. (*During the course of the following monologue, SOLDIER 2 interrupts his storytelling to correct audience members' positions*). What am I waiting for? When I was a kid, I was told I was worthless, that since I was not good in academics, I was good for nothing. No one ever asked me what I wanted to do or where I wanted to go...And then, in the eighth grade I watched the Bollywood movie *Border*. For the first time in my life, I was fascinated by the armed forces and that night when I went to bed, I had a dream. An incredible dream. An army of 300 brave Spartans charging over the enemy territory. The anger and blood in their eyes, the feeling of patriotism for their land. One among them — a young soldier —charging; making his way out to shed the blood of his enemy. Trrr...trrr.... trr...trrrrrrrrrrr... To fly, to wear the uniform, to do something for my land... So, when you ask me what I'm waiting for, well, I wait for the day a war breaks out and I get called to march ahead... I wait for the day I can shed every drop of my blood in serving my motherland and her boundaries, and when I come back from war, to continue my work to make this country a better place. It's this wait that keeps me alive. And all those people who told me I'm worthless, I'm waiting for the chance to prove them wrong.

SOLDIER #3: TURN TO ME. (*He smiles*) You don't have to do any exercises to hear my story.... Sit or stand how you like. What am I waiting for? I'm waiting for her. For her to come back to me and say to me that yes, she was wrong in her choice. I want her to feel that I was the best guy she could have ever met, and she made the biggest mistake of her life by choosing him. I am just waiting for the day that I will finish the Academy, become an officer, and go to her wearing that shining olive green uniform... Is that why she left me? Because I am an army man and she would have to be both the father and mother to our children?... I don't know. All I know is that I want her to regret choosing him. And he, he will realize that he too made the biggest mistake of his life by betraying such a good friend like me... What am I waiting for? I'm waiting for a true friend, true love. But what does this 'truth' look like? How does it behave? Do I ask for too much from the people in my life? I don't know... Maybe I'm asking for too much... (*Pause*) An army man getting desperate about a girl... You know, I think it's because I have too much time on my hands now. These peace postings, they give you too much time to think. Next week though, next week I'm being posted to Kashmir and then, I'm sure I'll forget all about the past. And I will find someone new. Someone better. I guess that's something worth waiting for!

SOLDIER #4: Turn to me, please. Please stand over there, in a line; thank you... What am I waiting for? You know, I wanted to become a doctor... or to just focus on buying a new car... or to start a chain of restaurants... but then, I got selected into the Academy... And now, now my life is so... screwed up. Running... 7 km, 10 km, 12 km, 20 km, punishments for minor mistakes, physical strength but intellectual degradation.... I am eagerly waiting for the day when I'll finish the Academy. I feel suffocated; like I'm caged in some kind of prison. But until that happens, I wait for the term break, count the days left to go home, clear my physical training tests, finish cross-country runs, try to clear my exams. Most of all, I wait to go home. For that day when I can wake up, pack my bags, check my tickets, get ready in jeans and a t-shirt, board the train, and leave the Academy. I close my eyes on the train and see people all around me, cheering, clapping. I'm playing on my guitar, performing to the words of my own life. Or, or, I'm sitting on a veranda with a good book, a hot cup of chai... (*Long pause*) You know what I'm waiting for? I'm waiting for the day that I have a child and then he or she gets to live their life their way. I'm waiting for my child to have the freedom and the independence that I... (*Pause*) Every day that passes by makes me think that I am a day closer to what I am waiting for. For the wait to be over.

SOLDIER 2: Ok, I'm bored with this storytelling now. Let's have some fun, guys, come on...

SOLDIERS #1, #2 & #3 stand up and start walking around the installation. They begin to play with the clothes that have been hung as part of the installation. Some of them caress the clothes that have been hung tenderly; others tear them down.

Each SOLDIER in this scene embodies a different approach to the armed forces.

How would you articulate the similarities and differences in their attitudes?

SOLDIER #4 conspicuously stands off to one side, not joining the others. SOLDIER #2 notices him after a while, goes to him, leads him to some of the clothes and tries to get him to play with the clothes as well. He tries for a few seconds but cannot seem to get into it the same way the others are. He watches the others for a while, wreaking havoc with the installation.

When their actions reach a frenzied pace, SOLDIER #4 pulls out a gun. Points it at his colleagues. Shoots them all. Puts the gun to his head. Freezes in position.

Silence.

While the SOLDIERS lie inert on the ground, the GUIDES and the ACTOR IN AUDIENCE involve the audience members in putting the clothes back in the way that they were when they first entered the room. Once some order has been restored:

GUIDE #1: Shall we move on, *janab?*

As the spectators begin to move toward the exit —

ACTOR
IN AUDIENCE: I can't, sir.

GUIDE #1: Why not?

ACTOR
IN AUDIENCE: I need to wait here. To make sure something is done about all of this.

GUIDE #1: About all of what?

ACTOR
IN AUDIENCE: What the soldiers have done here; something needs to be done about this. Him (*points to SOLDIER #4*)... how is shooting them and killing himself doing anything to change this situation?

GUIDE #1: You think he should have stopped them sooner?

ACTOR
IN AUDIENCE: He should have tried. Instead of just watching them do what they did and then taking out his anger in this way.

GUIDE #1: And if he had tried to stop them, what do you think would have happened?

ACTOR
IN AUDIENCE: They probably would have killed him. But he's dead either way, isn't he?

GUIDE #1: True. Whichever way he dies though, it doesn't stop what happened here.

ACTOR
IN AUDIENCE: That's why I can't continue on this journey, sir. I want to stay here. I want to wait and see that something is done about this.

GUIDE #1: People have already been waiting for a long time. It's the same old story. The people say, "They did this" and they say, "No we didn't." The cycle goes on. Your waiting here is not going to change anything.

ACTOR
IN AUDIENCE: You don't think I should try? Justice needs to be done and I want to help.

GUIDE #2: What does justice look like for something like this?

ACTOR
IN AUDIENCE: I don't know.

GUIDE #2: Is justice that the people who do this get put in prison?

ACTOR
IN AUDIENCE: Maybe.

GUIDE #2: Is justice that they get killed?

ACTOR
IN AUDIENCE: Maybe.

GUIDE #2: Is justice that the victims won't be ostracized anymore? That the women will finally start getting marriage proposals again?

ACTOR
IN AUDIENCE: Maybe.

GUIDE #2: Is justice that the victims will get a chance to take the perpetrators to court?

ACTOR
IN AUDIENCE: Maybe.

GUIDE #1: What is justice for something like this?

ACTOR
IN AUDIENCE: Maybe justice is that there will be no more weeping.

GUIDE #1: And if justice doesn't come today?

ACTOR
IN AUDIENCE: Maybe it will come tomorrow.

GUIDE #1: Or the day after tomorrow?

ACTOR
IN AUDIENCE: Possibly.

GUIDE #1: Until...?

ACTOR
IN AUDIENCE: Until justice comes.

ACTOR IN AUDIENCE sits down near the installation. A line of LABOURERS enter.

ACTOR
IN AUDIENCE: And who are you?

LABOURER: We were contracted to come and build this place back up sir.

> What are the identity politics that are introduced through the character of the LABOURER?

ACTOR
IN AUDIENCE: Of course. They couldn't get find any Kashmiri workers willing to come here so they brought you, isn't it?

LABOURER: I don't know, sir. We are here because we were told that we would make good money doing the construction here. We don't know anything about this place, and we don't want to get involved in the politics of what might be happening here.

ACTOR
IN AUDIENCE: You don't want to know about what happened here? You don't want to know why you've been asked to come here and build over this place?

LABOURER: No, sir.

ACTOR
IN AUDIENCE: You don't want to know?

LABOURER: No, sir. I am here to do my job. I am here to make money for my family. Please, just let me do what I was paid to do.

LABOURER moves ACTOR IN AUDIENCE out of the way and gives orders to his men to start the work. The men start singing a worker's song and pass bricks in a line. A wall is being built around the installation; ostensibly, to hide it from view. The ACTOR IN AUDIENCE gets more and more agitated till —

ACTOR
IN AUDIENCE: Stop. STOP DOING THIS.

LABOURER: What's your problem, man?

ACTOR
IN AUDIENCE: If you do this, if you build this wall, people will forget what happened here.

LABOURER: Maybe people want to forget what happened. What's wrong in that?

ACTOR
IN AUDIENCE: No, people should not forget. They cannot forget. You will not build anything here. This place needs to stay as it is as a reminder of what has happened. Of what continues to happen.

LABOURER: Look, I have a job to do and I need to do it. Please get out of my way.

LABOURER makes as if to start working again. The ACTOR IN AUDIENCE pulls audience members to stand in front of each labourer, while saying, "don't let him do anything, ok?"

The main LABOURER tries to stop ACTOR IN AUDIENCE by reasoning with him; reasoning with the audience members; raising his voice a little; calling his boss on his cell phone. But the ACTOR IN AUDIENCE continues doing what he's doing. Finally —

Look into the events that occurred in the town of Konun-Poshpora.

Consider the depiction of the events in this scene.

Consider how you might have approached the same events through the theatrical form.

LABOURER: PLEASE STOP THIS. HEY. STOP THIS. You are going to get me into a lot of trouble.

ACTOR
IN AUDIENCE: I don't care if you get in trouble. You are not changing anything here till justice comes. YOU WILL NOT CHANGE ANYTHING HERE TILL JUSTICE COMES.

Pause. The LABOURER realizes that this man is not going to get out of his way.

LABOURER: Come with me. Come and speak to my boss. You want us to stop building this wall? Come and talk to the man who actually makes the decision instead of taking out your frustration on us. Come on. Let's go.

The LABOURER ushers the ACTOR IN AUDIENCE toward the door and leaves the space with the other labourer's following him.

During the conversation that follows, the GUIDES also hand out a stone souvenir to each audience member. Each stone is covered with this information:

---

310 army personnel committed suicide since 2014: Government (*Hindustan Times*, 2017)

Indian army suicides blamed on 'poor leadership' (BBC, 2012)

Suicides and fratricide: Indian Army takes care of its soldiers, stop maligning it (Kakar, 2017).

Over 100 military personnel commit suicide every year (Pandit, 2017)

Why Are the Armed Forces in Kashmir Plagued by So Many Suicides and Fratricides? (Maqbool, 2017)

India's Troubled Soldiers (Ramachandran, 2013)

GUIDE #2: Every time I come to Kashmir I meet people who are fighting for what they believe in. People who are fighting for justice in their own way. And while there is a part of me that does understand their fights, I must admit that there is a part of me that remains uncertain. Uncertain of how all these different fights for justice will coalesce for Kashmir's future... I guess it's doesn't matter in the grand scheme of things, whether I understand or don't... Or does it matter? What do you think, *janab*?

GUIDE #1: Personally, I don't think it matters if you understand why people are fighting for justice in the way that they are. I don't think it even matters if I or other Kashmiris understand why a certain individual's fight for justice looks the way it does. What is important is that that person who is fighting understands why they are fighting the way they are fighting. It is important that that person understands what justice means to them and if/when their fight will be over.

GUIDE #2: But sir, what about how the fights all come together... For example, let's say this student here (*points to one member of the audience*) has found a way of fighting for justice that is completely different from what this other student (*points to another member of the audience*) thinks justice is. They both believe in their fights and their means. They both have their own definition of justice. But what does that mean in the larger scheme of things if one person's fight for justice derails another? What will that mean for the future of Kashmir?

GUIDE #1: That's a great question but one that I cannot answer. I daresay no one has been able to answer that question, have they?

GUIDE #2: No, no they haven't... So, shall we just move on then?

GUIDE #1: Shouldn't we wait to see what happens with this situation? If the young man who was protesting will find justice?

GUIDE #2: I think that will be a long wait, *janab*. Who knows what he will find and when he will find it.

GUIDE #1: You're right... Please, lead the way. Let' move on.

As the audience members move out from this space and into the next, they walk through a path made of sacks.

Scene Eight:
The Argumentation Cultures

▶ WATCH THE VIDEO

A CHORUS of PERSONS. As individual PERSONS speak, the CHORUS is in movement. Choreographed movement. There could be as few as one person in this CHORUS. Or as many as fifty.

PERSON: I really don't see why you have to be so negative all the time.

PERSON: I don't believe in foolish optimism.

PERSON: But what's the point of —

PERSON: I just don't believe in it. That's all.

PERSON: We need to talk about why you're so negative all the time.

PERSON: What makes you think I'm negative all the time?

PERSON: Well, every time I talk about a potential solution; about something that can be done, you seem to think that the solution won't work.

PERSON: Look, it's not that I don't think the solutions won't work, it's just... sometimes, when you provide solutions to problems that are so complex, it seems a bit... It seems, to me, like you might not have thought through the issues with that solution.

PERSON: DON'T BE SO NEGATIVE ALL THE DAMN TIME.

PERSON: DON'T TALK TO ME LIKE THAT. At least I'm not delusional, thinking that everything can be solved with —

PERSON: I am NOT DELUSIONAL. I have come up with ideas after a lot of thought —

PERSON: Looking for answers on Google does NOT count as research.

PERSON: Why do you have to be like this —

https://doi.org/10.11647/OBP.0223.14

PERSON: I'm not being like any —

PERSON: I have so much more experience that you in this particular issue. I've actually been there; I've spoken to people; I've dealt with important people. Have you read the literature about this subject? Have you seen what Fanon has to say about struggles for freedom? Let me give you an example of —

PERSON: You're not understanding what I'm saying to you. I don't know Fanon, but I know what Spivak says and let me tell you what —

PERSON: No, wait. Let me tell you my way of looking at things because I don't —

PERSON: NO IT"S MY TURN TO SPEAK AND I WANT TO BE HEARD FIRST.

PERSON: NO, YOU'RE MISUNDERSTANDING ME —

PERSON: Listen, listen. Just listen to — just listen —

PERSON: No... you're misunderstanding my point — listen...

PERSON: I admire your ability to critically question things, sir.

PERSON: I admire your ability to find solutions to problems.

> How does the content in this scene relate to the conflicts in Kashmir?
>
> How do 'argumentation cultures' function as a framework in exploring insider/ outsider dynamics within a particular context?

PERSON: Interesting idea...

PERSON: Will you be coming back tomorrow?

PERSON: Depends on the weather.

PERSON: It should be an interesting discussion.

PERSON: Perhaps.

PERSON: They'll talk about ideas like the one I just told you.

PERSON: Yes.

PERSON: So maybe I'll see you tomorrow.

PERSON: Maybe.

PERSON: Don't raise your voice when you are talking to people.

PERSON: Disagreements are a waste of time. If you meet someone who doesn't agree with you, just walk away.

PERSON: You need to tell people what you think. Be direct. Confront a problem head on.

PERSON: Sometimes you need to use your fists.

PERSON: It's best not to fight. People never change their minds.

PERSON: Make sure you are heard. Make sure your voice is heard.

PERSON: A hug solves everything.

PERSON: Just agree to disagree, no?

PERSON: Don't you dare argue with someone older than you.

PERSON: Don't argue with your husband.

PERSON: Stand your ground. Fight for what you believe in.

PERSON: It's always important to be polite.

PERSON: Act your age.

PERSON: You need to learn how to argue politely.

PERSON: I'm happy that we're looking to find ways to resolve this issue.

PERSON: Me too... I don't understand them, though.

PERSON: The arguing you mean?

PERSON: Yes! They were so... talking over each other all the time... Yelling.

PERSON: It was a bit loud...

PERSON: That can't be the way to resolve anything...

PERSON: "The" way, probably not. Maybe it's "a" way, though.

PERSON: I don't know... Seems impossible to me. I don't even know how to talk to them.

> How would you dramatize the ways in which arguments unfold in your community?

PERSON: Well, you're going to have to figure out a way... it's about time this thing got resolved.

PERSON: They're just so....

PERSON: Loud?

PERSON: No.

PERSON: Aggressive?

PERSON: No.

PERSON: Arrogant?

PERSON: No.

PERSON: Passionate?

PERSON: No...

PERSON: Committed?

PERSON: No.

PERSON: Argumentative?

PERSON: Different. They're just so... different... I don't know how to talk to them.

PERSON: Maybe you... maybe we need to learn?

PERSON: Can't they learn?

PERSON: Maybe this is why things never get done around here.

PERSON: Because they can't learn our way?

PERSON: And we can't learn theirs.

PERSON: So, things fall apart.

PERSON: So, things fall apart.

The CHORUS continues to move.

Design another exercise to get the audience to consider how the very way in which arguments are understood, might alter the way conflicts unfold.

GUIDE #1:[1] Some say that the long-standing conflict between Israeli Jews and Palestinian Arabs may be attributable, in part, to differences in communication styles. The Arab communication style is referred to as *musayra*, which means "to accommodate" or "to go along with," and is a communication pattern that orients the speakers toward harmonious social relations and a concern for face-saving. In contrast, the communication style used by Israeli Jews places an emphasis on assertiveness. This speech pattern is called *dugri*, which means "straight talk," and allows the free expression of the speaker's thoughts, opinions, or preferences that might pose a threat to the message receiver.

---

1   (Liu, 2016)

GUIDE #2: I want to ask you all to pair up with someone you don't know. I want you to talk to your partner about how you deal with a disagreement — do you shout? Do you run away from an argument? Do you hit the person who is arguing with you? Please, talk to each other about how you deal with a disagreement.

Audience member pairs are given time to discuss. The CHORUS continues to move among the audience members who are speaking. They stop occasionally. Listen to what is being said. Repeat aspects of what they hear.

A bell.

GUIDE #2: Now I want you to find someone else to talk to; someone else you don't know so well. And I want you to consider how you developed your argumentation style: is it from watching your parents fight? Is it from what your teachers told you in school? Why do you disagree with people in the way that you do?

Audience pairs are given time to discuss. The CHORUS continues to move among the audience members who are speaking. They stop occasionally. Listen to what is being said. Repeat what they hear. Maybe. Maybe not.

Through the second conversation, while the CHORUS moves, they hand stone souvenirs to each audience member. This time, the stone souvenir is covered with a very brief snapshot of Cockpit Culture Theory.[2]

A bell.

GUIDE #2: Let's come back together. Would anyone like to share something from what you discussed?

Audience members can talk if they wish. If the conversation goes on too long, the bell rings and GUIDE #2 takes them to the next space. If no one wants to speak, GUIDE #2 moves the group to the next space.

As audience members leave this space and walk to the next one, they walk down a path made of nails.

---

2   (Ohlheiser, 2013).

The First Coalition

The sections called COALITIONS are spaces of collaborative creation; a group of people coming together, albeit temporarily, to "make something": an atmosphere, a spirit, a hope, a recognition.

When spectators arrive at The First Coalition, the sign below greets them — under the sign, there is a display of the readings that they might choose from.

How would you articulate the difference between an INSTALLATION and a COALITION in *Chronicles from Kashmir*?

Choose one of these to read when we go inside.

The readings to choose from might include, but are not limited to:

Shahnaz Bashir's (2015) *A Bunker in Every Mind*

Jon Henley's (2016) report on Anders Breivik's appeal against human rights violations in Norway's prisons

Fabian Bosoer and Federico Finchelstein's (2014) *Argentina's Truth Commission at 30*

Freny Manecksha's (2014) *Autonomy Under Siege*

Asam Ahmad's (2015) *Bad Muslim*

Nawal El Saadawi's (2017) *Capitalism and Fundamentalism are Interdependent*

Extracts from Mahum Shabir's (2017) *Friday Notes on Kashmir*

Poems by Insha Muzafar (2017)

https://doi.org/10.11647/OBP.0223.15

Mediah Ahmed's (2016) *Mediah Visits the Inclusive Mosque*

Zulfikar Ali Bhutto's (2017) *Mussalmaan Musclemen: Dissecting Masculinity In Pakistan Through Art*

Nighat Sahiba's *Zard Paniek Dair* (Geelani, 2017)

Aga Shahid Ali's (2003) poems

Asad Hashim's (2011) *Kashmir in the Collective Imagination*

Habba Khatoon's (n.d.) *Why Are You Cross with Me?*

Some sheets of paper are intentionally blank, in case some spectators might prefer not to read. As each audience member picks their reading, they enter a room. In the centre of the room is a construction made of bricks and candles, with different documents contained between/ within the bricks and candles; documents that are visibly being burned. The pages being burned include extracts from the following reports:

Amnesty International's (2015) *Denied: Failures in Accountability in Jammu & Kashmir*

International People's Tribunal on Human Rights and Justice in Indian-administered Kashmir (2009) *Buried Evidence: Unknown, Unmarked, and Mass Graves in Indian-Administered Kashmir*

An IPTK and APDP Report (2015), *Structures of Violence: The Indian State in Jammu and Kashmir*

Once all the spectators have entered and are seated, the GUIDES invite the audience members to read the texts that they have chosen. The GUIDES act as facilitators, posing questions to the group when one text has been read. Asking them for interpretations and responses. Not asking them to look for ties between that text and Chronicles from Kashmir.

Once audience members have finished reading their chosen texts and begin to exit the space, there are loud sounds. Gunshots? Teargas shelling? Bombs?

The GUIDES rush the audience members back into the darkened space, where there is progressively less light. Two actors run into the space with the group: they are dishevelled; they lead the audience to understand that they have just run away from a violent demonstration; they talk to the audience about protests going on outside; they instruct them on the need for everyone to stay in the room for a little while.

This conversation is improvised. It is informal. It is realistic. There is no overt information given about the nature of the sounds or the violence. No one is quite sure what is happening; just that it is somewhere they should not be. There also does not have to be conversation.

There can just as well be silence.

After about 30 minutes of waiting; after about 30 minutes of being contained in that dark space, there is a garbled announcement. The GUIDES and actors inform the audience that it is now safe for them to leave.

The actors bid the audience farewell at this point and go on their own way.

The audience leaves the space and walks along a path lit by candles.

How can an audience be prepared for/warned about the ways in which the sounds of gunshots/teargas shelling/bombs might affect them?

While it would augment the impact of *Chronicles from Kashmir* not to forewarn audiences about the abovementioned sounds, different cultural contexts come with different needs for content warnings and advisories for spectators. How would you approach this kind of coalition, in your context?

Scene Nine: The Sikhs

A room with mirrors: like a green room. There should be, ideally, individual mirrors for each spectator.

Audience members at each mirror are assigned a MAKE-UP ARTIST. The GUIDES seat audience members at the different seats and then the MAKE UP ARTISTS take over. No talking. All that is heard is a song that has come to exemplify the presence of Sikhs in the Kashmir Valley.

As part of their make-up, audience members are given costumes — to wear over what they are wearing already, unless there is a changing room in that space for their transformation to take place expeditiously. Who do they become? Well, it's up to the MAKE-UP ARTISTS, isn't it?

Enter DIRECTOR, ASSISTANT DIRECTOR, CAMERA PEOPLE, and LIGHTING PERSONNEL (the latter are referred to as the crew at points in this scene).

While the DIRECTOR speaks, the others start setting up their equipment. It's a film shoot.

DIRECTOR: Are they all ready?

GUIDE #2: Yes, sir. I haven't had the chance to tell them what this is about —

> *The Sikhs* is one of the few scenes for which solely archival research was used.
>
> For all the other scenes, the content was created through a combination of archival research, interviews, conversations, and workshops.
>
> One of the goals in writing *The Sikhs*, therefore, was to visibly address the material's distance from lived experience.
>
> Can you identify the strategies that have been used to achieve these goals?

DIRECTOR: Right, let me do that then. So, we are here to shoot a film about some of the experiences of Sikhs in Kashmir. We're a little short of actors so that's why... well. You get the point. Now, most of our interviews are already done but we also want a few clips that are less... direct. Images that are more abstract... more conceptual.

We want to create a movie about the experiences of Sikhs in Kashmir, but we also want to make it in a way that is... (*he gesticulates with his arms, trying to find the right words*). Look, bottom line: you all don't have to worry about a thing. We will tell you exactly what you need to do. Yes?

https://doi.org/10.11647/OBP.0223.16

The sequence of images that follow are deliberately described by content, rather than form. Based on the number of spectators and based on the space available, the construction of the images should differ. What is necessary though, is that the topic of each image is maintained.

The images can be understood as a tableau. A still image.

In these images, the DIRECTOR arranges the audience members into a particular composition and asks them to remain frozen in that position until he tells them that they can move.

Once the audience members are in the position desired by the DIRECTOR, the ASSISTANT DIRECTOR, CAMERA PEOPLE, and LIGHTING PERSONNEL take a short (1-minute) video of that particular image.

After each image has been filmed, audience members are told to relax, and immediately the recording is shown to the DIRECTOR on a screen that is also visible to the audience. The audience must be able to watch the recording as well.

After each recording is shown, the DIRECTOR and the ASSISTANT DIRECTOR have a brief conversation about the product. Sometimes, they want to reshoot an image because something hasn't been communicated accurately. Sometimes, they are happy with an image. Sometimes, they absolutely disagree on an image and have to either agree to disagree or to discard that image all together.

IMAGE #1: The Sikhs as a unique minority in the Kashmir Valley

After IMAGE #1 is staged, the DIRECTOR tells the audience to freeze in that position. The crew films that image for 1 minute. The video is played back for the DIRECTOR and the people in the image.

DIRECTOR: Yes, that works. That looks good to me. Anyone disagree?

ASSISTANT
DIRECTOR: Looks fine, sir. Looks fine.

DIRECTOR: Good. Let's move to the next one then. Let's see... It's the floods one. Let's bring in the props, please?

IMAGE #2: The Sikh community helping those affected during the 2014 floods, with the distribution of food and medicines

The necessary props are set up by the crew members and once IMAGE 2 is staged, the crew takes a video of the image for 1 minute. The video is played back for the DIRECTOR and the people in the image:

ASSISTANT
DIRECTOR: Something is missing sir.

DIRECTOR: What do you think?

ASSISTANT
DIRECTOR: I think that prop doesn't work for this scene, sir. It's too direct and obvious. Can we use something more abstract?

DIRECTOR: What did you have in mind?

ASSISTANT
DIRECTOR: It needs more texture, I think, sir. The trough. Maybe we can use the trough and fill it with —

DIRECTOR: Yes, I love that idea. Do it.

ASSISTANT DIRECTOR and the crew bring in a trough (audience can be asked to help). The trough is filled with water. Excited that the suggestion has been accepted enthusiastically, the ASSISTANT DIRECTOR starts to compose the image. Midway through this, the DIRECTOR interrupts the ASSISTANT DIRECTOR and rearranges elements of the image. From an image that was more abstract, the DIRECTOR chooses realism. The ASSISTANT DIRECTOR is visibly dissatisfied. This dissatisfaction is ignored by the DIRECTOR.

IMAGE #2 is recorded as the DIRECTOR sets it up. The video is shown again.

This time, while other members of the crew point out to things they like about the image, ASSISTANT DIRECTOR stays quiet.

DIRECTOR: Well?

ASSISTANT DIRECTOR shrugs.

DIRECTOR: Don't sulk. If you have something to say, say it.

ASSISTANT DIRECTOR shrugs again.

DIRECTOR: Fine, let's just proceed.

IMAGE #3: Interfaith partnerships, but not interfaith marriages

Before IMAGE #3 is completed by the DIRECTOR —

ASSISTANT
DIRECTOR: Sir —

DIRECTOR: Now you want to say something?

ASSISTANT
DIRECTOR: Sir, it's just —

How do you interpret the topic for Image #3?

What does this topic tell you about the intracultural dynamics between the communities in question?

DIRECTOR: Just say it!

ASSISTANT
DIRECTOR: Sir, this image is too vague, sir.

DIRECTOR: First the images are too obvious, and now they're too vague? Do you want
to direct this?

ASSITANT
DIRECTOR: No sir, I just — It's ok, sir. Please go ahead as you wish.

DIRECTOR is irritated.

*After IMAGE #3 is staged, the crew films it for 1 minute. The video is played back for the
DIRECTOR and the people in the image:*

DIRECTOR: Well?

ASSITANT
DIRECTOR: It's fine, sir.

DIRECTOR: You don't like it.

ASSISTANT
DIRECTOR: It's OK.

DIRECTOR: Go on, do it your way and show me.

*ASSISTANT DIRECTOR changes the image and this time, attempts to create a "sense" of the
protest but without the placards. IMAGE #3 is restaged, reshot, and shown once again. The
ASSISTANT DIRECTOR is visibly nervous. Keen to make their point, yes. But nervous.*

*The DIRECTOR pulls up two videos of IMAGE #3 together. The two videos are shown side by
side and the DIRECTOR turns to one of the audience members:*

DIRECTOR: Which one do you prefer? (*Listens to audience response and regardless of what
is said*) Let's keep both for now and choose later, yes?

ASSISTANT
DIRECTOR: Sure, sir.

DIRECTOR: OK, next image. Which one is that?

ASSISTANT
DIRECTOR: The triangle one, sir.

DIRECTOR: Right... Let's see. (*Turns to GUIDES*) We'll need you both for this one.

IMAGE #4: A triangle between Pandits, Muslims, and Sikhs

After IMAGE #4 is staged, the crew films it for 1 minute. The video is played back for the DIRECTOR and the people in the image.

DIRECTOR: No, I don't like this one. It creates this... makes a problematic comparison between two different communities... Let's try something else.

After IMAGE #4 is restaged, the crew takes another video of it. The video is played back for the DIRECTOR and the people in the image.

DIRECTOR: (*To GUIDE #1*) What do you think, sir?

GUIDE #1: I don't know... something seems missing. What are you trying to say with this image?

DIRECTOR: I want to show something about how the Pandits, Sikhs, and Muslims have interacted in the Valley... that there are different ways in which they have evolved... that it's tough to figure out why one set of relationships worked out one way, while the other didn't....

GUIDE #1: I... maybe one of our visitors will have an idea sir?

Audience members are given the chance to give suggestions that the DIRECTOR can try, or not. If there are no suggestions from the audience, the GUIDES can give ideas. If they have none either, the DIRECTOR says he will think about it later and moves on to the next image.

DIRECTOR: Let's move on to the last one. For this, everyone, I need to move turbans from over there and place them in rows. (*Audience members are shown how to do this*).

IMAGE #5: A memorial of Sikh martyrs, who have played a role in Kashmir's history

After IMAGE #5 is staged, the crew films it.

The video is played back for the DIRECTOR and the people in the image. The DIRECTOR and ASSISTANT DIRECTOR both like this image.

> Which historical event in Kashmir might Image #5 be referencing?
>
> Why has the name of the event been obscured from the text?

DIRECTOR: Ok, that's a wrap. Thank you all for helping. You can get out of your costumes now and we'll have some tea and snacks served as a small thank-you for your help! If you would like a copy of the images, please let one of them (*points to the GUIDES*) know and we'll get a copy to you.

ASSITANT
DIRECTOR: If you have any questions after you get out of your costume, please come

chat with us. We'll be over there (*points to a corner*) editing the video.

The DIRECTOR and crew remain in a corner, looking at the footage. Audience members work with the make-up artists again and once they are back in their everyday clothes, they can choose to speak to the DIRECTOR and the crew about any questions they have about the images of which they were part.

The same song that played in the beginning plays at the end. Tea and biscuits are provided to the audience as a thank-you from the film crew.

During the tea break, the DIRECTOR and other crew members thank each audience member and hands them a stone souvenir that is wrapped with an image that documents Sikhs living in Kashmir.

Which lesser-known voices in Kashmir would you want to add to the passageway that is described as linking the space containing this scene to the one that follows?

Once audience members are out of their costumes, have had their tea break, and have received their souvenir, the GUIDES take them to the next space down a path that is made up of visuals of lesser-known Kashmiri voices. Voices from the Gujjars, or from Kashmir's LGBTQI+ community.

But also, possibly, more conceptual imagery that alludes to voices of everyday inequalities that are inevitably glossed over amidst the more spectacular narrative of war.

Scene Ten: The Apples

 WATCH THE VIDEO

ACTORS — as many or as few as needed — form a circle with GUIDES #1 & #2 and the audience members. Each person is given an apple. An ACTOR speaks.

ACTOR: Use the apple to express yourself.

An ACTOR uses their apple as a stone.

Applause.

ACTOR: Use the apple to express yourself.

Pause for a few seconds. If no audience members step in,

Another ACTOR puts their apple on top of their head and walks to the other side of the circle.

Applause.

ACTOR: Use the apple to express yourself.

Pause for a few seconds. If no audience members step in,

Another ACTOR walks into the middle of the circle. Takes a bite. Spits it out.

Applause.

ACTOR: Use the apple to express yourself.

Pause for a few seconds. If no audience members step in,

Another ACTOR takes a chair from somewhere in the room and puts the apple on it.

Applause.

ACTOR: Use the apple to express yourself.

> Each performer in the video has used the apple differently.
>
> Which performer's approach affected you the most? Why?

https://doi.org/10.11647/OBP.0223.17

Pause for a few seconds. If no audience members step in,

GUIDE #2 pounds the apple on the floor.

Applause.

> What do the apples symbolize, to you?

ACTOR: Use the apple to express yourself.

Once all audience members and ACTORS who want to participate have done so, GUIDE #1 steps in. GUIDE #1 should be the last one to participate.

> If you were a performer/ spectator in this scene, how would have used an apple?

GUIDE #1 takes a bite of the apple. Then, he takes the apple to someone else in the circle and asks that person to take a bite from it. Then, he takes the apple to another person, and asks them to now take a bite from the same apple. GUIDE #1 gestures to the others in the circle — they can share their apples too. To him, expressions of the self cannot happen without a confluence of forces; without convergence; without overlaps.

ACTORS give each audience member a stone souvenir that is covered with a step by step guide on how to write a manifesto. Something like: How to Write Your Manifesto In 5 Steps (Grammarly, 2014).

Once all audience members have a stone souvenir, a moment. Then, all the ACTORS exit.

GUIDE # 2: Let's move on?

When the audience members are led out of this space and into the next one, they walk down a path that is installed with microphones.

INSTALLATION C

The general instructions that introduce INSTALLATION A also apply here. The exhibits below are described in no particular order — each one will, ultimately, have to be installed as best fits the chosen site.

Before the audience enters the space:

GUIDE #1: Before we enter this space, there is something that I would like to share with you all. I know you might be tired by now. Walking around these different spaces. Encountering different kinds of pain in each one. I wouldn't blame you if you were tired. Perhaps even a bit... bored?

(*Pause*)

War is not always about the bombs. Or the curfews. Or the spectacular stories of protest. War is also banal. Ordinary. Boring. So, experience the tiredness. The exhaustion. The boredom. Notice the ways in which your mind becomes numb — exhausted — from hearing one more story about pain and suffering. Feel those responses with every pore of your being. Maybe, then, you will understand just a little bit more about Kashmir.

Long pause. GUIDE #1 looks the audience in the eye.

GUIDE #2: Shall we?

GUIDE #1: Please.

They enter the space.

Exhibit #1: Gallery

This gallery is an image-based exposition of Kashmiri stone-pelters and the police, drawn from a Reuters' photo essay on the theme (McNaughton & Bukhari, 2017). The display of photographs is interspersed with text, also drawn from the article. Something like this:

> What are the effects of placing images of stone-pelters and police officers alongside each other?

 https://doi.org/10.11647/OBP.0223.18

Photograph of Stone-Pelter	Photograph of Kashmiri Police Officer
Text	Text
Photograph of Stone-Pelter	Photograph of Kashmiri Police Officer
Text	Text
Photograph of Stone-Pelter	Photograph of Kashmiri Police Officer
Text	Text

Exhibit #2: Word Cluster

The following words are displayed, in whatever fashion best fits the space.

Ikhwan Armed militia that are sponsored by the Indian government

Civilians
Traitors
Protesters
Stone-pelters
Activists
Dissidents
Separatists
Sympathizers
Collaborators
Ikhwans

Exhibit #3: Activity

The instruction below is posted for the audience. Near the instruction are cups, each of which are tagged with a particular concept or theme. The audience is invited to use the wool provided for them, to make connections between the highlighted concepts and themes.

Use the wool to make connections.

What concepts/themes
you would add/delete
from those that are
already listed to be
included on the cups?
Why?

Suggested concepts and themes for the cups:

Obedience	Discipline	Created	Agency
Nationalism	Language	Forgotten	Press
Commercialism	Tradition	Secularism	Violence
Incarceration	Migration	Rebellion	Disappeared
Conditions	Displaced	Masculinity	The Banal
Civil Society	Militants	Soldiers	Nation
Victim	Perpetrator	Grey Zone	Autonomy
Femininity	Hope	Sexual Assault	Puppet
Memory	Violence	Justice	Similarities
Collateral	Truth	Power	Development
Hierarchy	Reparations	Responsibility	Security
History	Militarization	Forward	Inaccessible
Religion	Difference	Peace	Transparency

Exhibit #4: Buzzfeed Booth

A poster of the Bollywood movie *Haider* is pasted alongside a screening of the same film; the audio comes through speakers and in so doing, becomes the soundscape for the installation space. There should be comfortable seating spaces in front of the screening, allowing spectators to rest and simply watch the video, should they desire to do so.

Suggested Menu for this Installation Space

Salty chai (*Noon chai*) and Kashmiri breads.

Stone Souvenir

During the installation, just as in the preceding scenes, the GUIDES give spectators a souvenir to carry in their bags. Here, the souvenir is a stone that has wrapped around it a piece of paper containing the following text:

Experiences like *Chronicles from Kashmir* blur lines between a theatrical setting and an educational environment (like a classroom).

What are the benefits/limitations of that boundary-blurring?

Walking around these different spaces. Encountering different kinds of pain in each one. I wouldn't blame you if you were tired. Perhaps even a bit... bored?

I hope you are tired. Because, maybe, if this one day of journeying through Kashmir's different stories is exhausting for you, you might be able to imagine what it's like for us...

War is not always about bombs.
Or curfews.
Or spectacular stories of protest.
War is also banal —
Ordinary.
Boring.

So, experience the tiredness. The exhaustion. The boredom.

Notice the ways in which your mind becomes numb — exhausted — from hearing one more story about pain and suffering.

Feel those responses with every pore of your being.

Maybe, then, you will understand just a little bit more about Kashmir.

After 30 minutes, the GUIDES ask the audience to follow them to the next location. As the audience exits this space and moves on to the next one, they walk along a path that is designed using woollen webs.

The Second Coalition

Like the ones that came before it, this COALITION is a space of collaborative creation; of a group of people coming together, albeit temporarily, to "make something": an atmosphere, a spirit, a hope, a recognition.

A pool of water. A lake. A river. Something. Young children are playing in the water, jumping around, swimming. Boys, mostly. Maybe there's one girl? A "tomboy"? Can that happen?

The audience is invited to join these children in their play.

A picnic is hosted on the banks of that body of water. The audience eats. Rests. Plays.

After all, even in war zones, children play.

When there has been a time of rest and play, the children lead the audience members by the hand down the next path, to the next space, where they bid them farewell. A path made of swings where, if the audience members choose to, they can continue their play.

> Why include a dimension of "play" in an experience like
> *Chronicles from Kashmir*?

> How would you train actors for a coalition like this one?
>
> Would they be themselves, the actors?
>
> Or would they craft characters for these scenes?

  https://doi.org/10.11647/OBP.0223.19

Scene Eleven:
The Village-City Love Affair

▶ WATCH THE VIDEO

As the audience members come close to this space, the GUIDES "shush" them in a mischievous way. It's like they are children playing a game; a game of hide and seek, perhaps?

The audience members watch the first part of the following scene through windows. Through curtains. Through something that makes what they're doing surreptitious — clandestine — the audience are watching a couple. A young Kashmiri woman (WIFE) from the city; a young Kashmiri man (HUSBAND) from the countryside.

The couple is inside a kitchen and what is happening, is nothing remarkable. In fact, it is the most normal thing many can think of. The young woman is at the stove, making a lot of food. There is music in the background; soft, romantic.

The man is setting up spaces for people to eat. It seems that they are expecting a lot of guests. He sets out plates and glasses of water; two dastarkhaans. *Once he is done, he walks up to the woman. Stands behind her while she cooks. She feeds him something from the dish she is preparing — he eats out of her hand. A moment of beautiful intimacy. Quiet love.*

> *Dastarkhaans*
> Long cloth that is set on the floor/table in order to serve food

A door slams inside the house. Another man walks in. The couple immediately move apart and the husband continues with his set-up of the space. The man who has just entered is the man's BROTHER. He looks like he has been hard at work.

He sits near the food; HUSBAND sits next to him. WIFE turns the music down and gives the BROTHER water/chai/something to drink. From the non-verbal interactions thus far, it should be obvious that there is some tension in the room. After a minute or so of silence:

https://doi.org/10.11647/OBP.0223.20

BROTHER: When are they coming?

WIFE: Any minute now.

Pause.

HUSBAND: How was it today?

BROTHER: Fine.

Pause.

HUSBAND: Did you get the package you were waiting for?

BROTHER: Not yet.

This scene seeks to highlight intracultural differences between Kashmiris (drawing from Bharucha, 2003) rather than intercultural ones between Kashmiris and non-Kashmiris.

Consider how intracultural dynamics manifest in the community in which you live.

What are the multiple cultural contexts that are contained within an otherwise cohesive identity grouping?

What do intracultural understandings reveal, as compared to intercultural dynamics?

Pause.

BROTHER: Did you hear what happened in Srinagar today?

HUSBAND: No.... we've been preparing for the guests all day.

BROTHER: They were supposed to protest at the University...

HUSBAND: And?

BROTHER: Nothing... they cancelled it at the last minute.

WIFE: Must have been some deal between them.

BROTHER: Who hasn't made a deal here.

HUSBAND: Please don't start. The guests are coming soon.

Pause. Everyone is agitated.

BROTHER: All I want to say is —

WIFE: Yes, I know what you want to say.

BROTHER: Why don't you let me finish —

WIFE: I get it. You people from the village are the true revolutionaries. Us city people do nothing but sit around all day.

BROTHER: That's not what I said —

WIFE: It's what you meant.

HUSBAND: Shabnam, please —

WIFE: I've had enough of your brother telling me what city people are like.

HUSBAND: He's just trying to —

WIFE: You don't need to explain to me. I know.

Voices become raised, with the WIFE repeating at various volumes (while also cooking) the ways in which the BROTHER's biases keep affecting her experience in their family.

BROTHER and HUSBAND are trying to remedy the situation but are unable to get a word in edgewise. This is the WIFE's rant and she's letting them have it. They eventually look bashful. And lapse into silence.

As the tension builds inside the room, the GUIDES signal to each other — and, feeling awkward for having the guests watch this family dynamic through the windows, they decide to knock on the door. WIFE, HUSBAND, and BROTHER immediately stop talking. Their attention shifts to the guests.

It becomes apparent through the HUSBAND, BROTHER, and WIFE's shift in behaviour that the audience is the group that they have been expecting for dinner.

GUIDE #1 sits with the women and WIFE around one of the eating areas; GUIDE #2 sits with the men, BROTHER, and HUSBAND around another of the eating areas.

As the food is being prepared and served, GUIDE #1 and GUIDE #2 talk to the hosts about how their days have been. They ask, diplomatically, if everything is all right, since they heard raised voices coming from the room. WIFE, BROTHER, and HUSBAND say that there is nothing to worry about.

The food is served, and it is clear that the hosts have been asked to prepare Kashmiri food for the GUIDES' guests to try. They serve one or two traditional dinner dishes and explain the contents of those dishes while they are being served; yakhni should be part of the menu.

> *Yakhni*
> A yogurt-based dish that is particular to Kashmiri cuisine

While the audience members are eating, HUSBAND, WIFE, and BROTHER ask them questions about where they are from. What brought them to Kashmir? What have they seen so far? What is food like where they come from?

Audience members are welcome to ask the performers questions as well.

If conversation runs out, people eat in silence. There is still music playing.

Once everyone is close to being done with the food, maybe when noon chai *is being served:*

GUIDE #2: So, I should tell you all why I brought you here for dinner. Shabnam was one of the first people that I met in Srinagar — she wasn't married then... (*everyone smiles*). We met through my colleague here, actually (*points to GUIDE #1*) and when Shabnam heard that I had never tried *yakhni*, she invited me to her house the next day and with her family, I enjoyed my first taste of this dish... Shabnam was instrumental in educating me about Kashmiri food and so now, whenever I guide a group like you, I bring them to meet Shabnam and taste her food... (*GUIDE #2 turns to the WIFE*) Do you want to tell them the story or should I?

The stories are shared informally, conversationally. It is talk between friends who have just shared food together; it is not a "performance."

WIFE: I can tell the story... So, when he came to my house that day, my parents were telling him about how *yakhni* was the reason they got married... (*She smiles*). They had an arranged marriage — my parents — and on the day that my father's family went to meet my mother and her family for the first time, she had prepared *yakhni* for them. When my grandfather came back home and described my mother's *yakhni* to my father... he says he had no choice but to agree to marry her. (*WIFE, HUSBAND, and BROTHER smile*). So now, any time they have a fight, she makes him *yakhni*; as a way to remember that day....

HUSBAND: *Yakhni* is the last dish to be served in our Kashmiri *wazwaan* and it has brought even the most nefarious wrestlers onto the right path (*he smiles*).

GUIDE #2: It's amazing how many memories have something to do with food, no? Sir, (*looking over at GUIDE #1*), what's the most powerful memory you have associated with food?

GUIDE #1 smiles.

GUIDE #1: Too many to tell you about now.

GUIDE #2: Tell us about one? Something from your childhood, perhaps?

Pause.

GUIDE #1: Hmmm.... (*he takes a few seconds to think*). So, when I was young... 10 or 11 years old, maybe. I can't really remember umm... anyway, we lived in the city at that time. My father had a government job and was posted there. And when we went to the city for the first time, I remember thinking that I would never fit in. So much noise. So much activity. We were village folk, you know?

(*A pointed look is exchanged between WIFE, BROTHER, and HUSBAND*).

One day I was walking home from school with my brother... or was it my sister? One of them. Maybe it was my... anyway, that's not important. So, we were walking home from school, and I saw this old man at his shop... He was making... I can't even remember now what he was making.

What I do remember though, is that he called me into his shop and gave me some of the food he was making as a treat... the smell inside that shop was so... It smelled like home, to me. And for the first time, in the city, I felt at home. I know this doesn't directly answer your question but —

GUIDE #2: No, no, you answered my question just fine.

Pause.

GUIDE #2 points to someone in the audience who has been happy to participate from the beginning; someone who does not seem like they will be too uncomfortable at being asked to speak.

GUIDE #2: What's your favourite memory associated with food?

Audience member is given a chance to respond. If the person called upon to respond says something, great. If not, the conversation is allowed to unfold till it seems to reach a natural conclusion.

GUIDE #2: OK, Shabnam. I think it's time for us to go now. Thank you so much.

WIFE: Are you sure you don't want some more tea or something before you go?

GUIDE #2: We would love to stay but you know we have to take these folks to as many places as we can before they leave.

WIFE, HUSBAND, and BROTHER shake hands with each audience member and, as a goodbye gift, give each of them a stone souvenir that is wrapped in beautiful paper containing a quotation. Something like this:

> Perhaps, instead of interculturalism, what we need in India is a stronger awareness of our intracultural affinities. It is only by respecting the specificities of our "regional" cultures that we in India can begin to understand how much we have in common. (Bharucha, 2003:39)

When the GUIDES lead the audience members to the next space, they are on a path made of wooden planks. A bridge, perhaps?

As you can see in this video, scenes from *Chronicles* are set in physical spaces that contain the same function as those in the script, i.e., scenes that take place in toilets are staged in toilets; scenes that take place in kitchens take place in kitchens. This aesthetic choice holds true in both the live and filmed versions of this work.

But, like any creative work, different decisions might be made.

So, what if you were asked to produce/direct *Chronicles from Kashmir* in an auditorium rather than as a site-responsive promenade piece?

How would such a decision alter the particularities of this creation?

A WEDDING and
a CURFEWED NIGHT

WATCH THE VIDEO

The Wedding

WATCH THE VIDEO

The Curfewed Night, Part 1

WATCH THE VIDEO

The Curfewed Night, Part 2

Given the nature of this scene, their filmed versions have been intentionally left without subtitles.

Follow the actors' physicality and their vocalization.

The text was entirely improvised anyway.

Given the complexity of the tasks involved in this eight-hour section of the experience, the format below has been chosen to give the reader a clear idea of what is to unfold. For an even more rigorous breakdown, please see the timeline that has been included at the end of the script.

***

Duration: 1 hour and 10 minutes

The audience reaches a home where a wedding is underway. Spectators are offered traditional Kashmiri tea and actors speak with them, in their roles as members of a wedding party.

  https://doi.org/10.11647/OBP.0223.21

| Mehandi |
| Henna |
| |
| Raat |
| Night |

This event is the *mehandi raat* and is a ceremony in which the groom's little finger is decorated with henna. The next morning, the groom traditionally goes to the bride's home, to bring her back. A cake is cut during this night; there is dancing and singing. The groom's friends are the ones who lead the festivities. The groom's father — the head of the household — coordinates all the events.

Halfway through this time period, a curfew is announced outside. While there is still celebration in the air, the atmosphere in the house changes because of the curfew. The curtains are drawn. Music plays, but the volume is low.

Audience members are asked to help members of the home with tasks (since more guests are supposedly *en route* and plans have had to be changed because of the curfew). Spectators help with decorating the space; arranging the bedding; cooking; taking photographs. The audience members should be made to feel like part of the wedding — it should also enable them to talk to the actors informally; to share what they have seen in the performance thus far; the questions that they have.

Neighbours interrupt from time to time, asking the wedding party to keep their voices down. Maybe there's an occasional sound of protests; of teargas shelling; of pellet guns.

Toward the end of this time frame, the groom is brought in, there is song and dance; celebrations reach a peak.

***

Duration: 40 minutes

In the midst of the celebration, there is banging at the door. A man, injured by pellets fired by the Indian army, runs in and wants to hide. Some actors playing the wedding hosts rush the pellet victim to another space, where the guests won't have to see him. Others talk about how to take the injured person to hospital, but no one is ready to risk his life due to the restrictions outside.

Suddenly a few army men enter the house and start asking about the injured man. They spill all the arranged sweets, pull out the clothes that are there, and start an identification parade of all the family members — guests and locals are separated for this. The army officers start searching all the rooms, drag out the pellet-injured man from the room, and take him along with them.

All the family, friends, and guests, after a shock, start rearranging the sweets and redo the arrangements for the *mehandi raat*. After re-settling the arrangements, the head of the family directs the groom to prepare for the *mehandi*.

A decorated cake is brought out and put on the table. There is a *wanvun* in the background. The groom is made to sit on a stage. His feet and hands are washed. The mother of the groom applies *mehandi* to the little finger of his right hand. The mother of the groom also applies *mehandi* for the groom's friends and other guests. Now sweets are distributed among the guests.

> *Wanvun*
> A style of choral singing that is particular to Kashmir

Then, the groom cuts the cake; he takes a bite of it, then it is cut into pieces, and distributed among the friends and guests. The sweets are also distributed among the guests.

Since the curfew is still underway, mattresses are laid out in a space, and the GUIDES ask audiences to get some rest while they go out and try to figure out how to continue the tour amidst the curfew. Once the GUIDES leave the space, a projector turns on and the following images/events take place within that framework. Audience members are welcome to stay awake or to sleep for a bit.

***

Duration: 8 hours
Hour 1
20 minutes of static

20 minutes of a special light on an actor
> For these twenty minutes, this actor has one primary action: tweezing the hair on his face. As he does so, he looks into a mirror; looks at his reflection. Each hair that he tweezes, has a story; a voice. A story that only he knows.

> ACTOR: *tweezes hair, looks at it*

> *tweezes hair, looks at it*

> *tweezes another hair, looks at it*

> *tweezes another hair, looks at it*

> *He keeps tweezing.*

> *At some point, another actor comes in and starts threading his face till tears are rolling down his face.*

20 minutes of a "guest"
> The "guest" appears through Skype; through a documentary video; through screenings of existing artistic responses/commentaries to particular wars in other contexts. This video has a single objective: to place Kashmir amidst global struggles for autonomy; to provide nuanced perspectives about the place for an outsider in these contexts; contemplations about who the outsider might be.

In this hour, the "guest video" should focus on Palestine.

***

Hour 2
20 minutes of static

20 minutes of a special light on an actor
> For these twenty minutes, this actor has one primary action: applying henna, like nail polish, on her hand and toenails. It is a ritual; something she does every day. And in its banality, in being utterly commonplace; she is a vision.

> ACTOR: a*pplies henna to one nail, looks at it*

>   *applies henna to one nail, looks at it*

>   *applies henna to one nail, looks at it*

>   *applies henna to one nail, looks at it*

>   *She keeps applying the henna.*

20 minutes of a "guest"
> In this hour, the "guest video" should focus on Kurdistan.

***

Hour 3
20 minutes of static

20 minutes of a special light on an actor
> During this time, the actor's phone is paired with the projector. We see him/her chatting with a Facebook account. Someone who talks to them, asks personal questions, disappears for a minute or two, before coming back and asking more questions. At one point, once intimate details have been revealed, the person on the other end of the Facebook chat, attempts to blackmail the actor; asking to be paid money in order to keep their secrets. The vignette culminates with the actor attempting to discern the identity of the person they are speaking with.

20 minutes of a "guest"
> In this hour, the "guest video" should focus on the Zapatistas.

***

Hour 4
20 minutes of static

20 minutes of a special light on an actor
   The actor repeatedly does the *nimaaz*; even
   though it might not be the right time for it

20 minutes of a "guest"
   In this hour, the "guest video" should focus on
   Somaliland

> *Nimaaz*
> The ritualistic prayer that
> is performed by Muslims
> five times a day

> What are the implications
> of invoking religious
> practices, like the *nimaaz*,
> within the framework of
> theatrical performance?

***

Hour 5
20 minutes of static

20 minutes of a special light on an actor
   During this time, the actor makes *chai*, arranges snacks, and hands them out to
   spectators who are awake

20 minutes of a "guest"
   In this hour, the "guest video" should focus on East Timor.

***

Hour 6
20 minutes of static

20 minutes of a special light on an actor
   The actor listens to a Kashmiri musician; someone old; someone unforgotten

20 minutes of a "guest"
   In this hour, the "guest video" should focus on Tibet

***

Hour 7
20 minutes of static

20 minutes of a special light on an actor
   During this time, the actor's phone is paired with the projector. We see him/her
   chatting and engaging with articles on news sites: looking at a story and posting
   a diatribe about it. Engaging, then, in conversational comments with people who
   agree/disagree with the actor's post

20 minutes of a "guest"
    In this hour, the "guest video" should focus on Kosovo

***

Hour 8
20 minutes of static

20 minutes of a special light on an actor, while s/he sleeps

20 minutes of nothing

***

In live performances of *Chronicles from Kashmir*, in order to sustain the sheer duration of this scene, the actors could be versions of themselves. They could keep their own names and lived experiences; they only needed to change their relationship to the situation.

So, Syed — the actor playing the character of the bridegroom — could be called Syed during *A Wedding and a Curfewed Night*. He could answer impromptu questions from the audience based on his own lived experience. The only aspect that needed to change was that Syed, for the duration of this scene, had to be a bridegroom.

This particular actor-character blend worked for us because EKTA's performers had the lived experience of the characters in the script. However, if *Chronicles from Kashmir* were to be staged with performers who do not have that lived experience, how might they be trained? Are scripts like *Chronicles from Kashmir* simply not meant for performers who do not have the lived experience in question? Or, is there a different choice that might be made in order to involve performers without the relevant lived experience? Like, for instance, setting *Chronicles from Kashmir* in a world of speculative fiction, rather than that of a South Asian reality?

What kind of speculative fictitious world would you create for *Chronicles from Kashmir*?

Duration: 40 minutes

The GUIDES walk in, turn on the radio, and begin setting out some food. The audience members are woken up by the GUIDES, who tell each of spectators that the curfew has been lifted, and that they should gather their energy before continuing on with their journey.

Audience members are given time to freshen up and eat before leaving the wedding household. The hosts of the wedding give each audience member a little bag with souvenirs, one of which is a stone that is covered with text about weddings in war zones (like Harris, n.d.).

As the audience members are led out of this curfewed night and into the next space, they have to navigate through a path made of barbed wire.

In addition to the challenge of actors needing to remain in character for an extended duration, the challenge of scenes like *A Wedding and a Curfewed Night* is how to maintain the stakes.

How do you get an audience to buy into the stress of a curfew, while knowing that they are — in reality — safe?

How can the audience be made to experientially understand the gravity of a situation, without blurring the lines between their own realities and fictions?

Scene Twelve: The Mirrors & a Poetic Lament

A room full of mirrors.

The text, punctuation marks, and spaces — everything below can be staged as the directors see fit.

But the mirrors need to be used.

I wish I could
          I can't
                I wish he would
                     He won't
                          Should I?
                             May I?
                                  Won't I?

At every night's end
I pull out my phone and look at the news.
I read.
Re-read.
Search.
Discover.
Maybe it's someone I know?

                              At every night's end
                I pull out my laptop and look at the news.
                                     I read.
                                Re-read.
                                Search.
                            Discover.
             Maybe it's someone I know?

https://doi.org/10.11647/OBP.0223.22

I call.

I listen.
I speak.

I search.

It could always be someone I know.

Every time there is the most miniscule shift
The haziest of blurs
The subtlest of signs

Everything stops.

I sit up.
Hoping against hope,
that it is not one of mine.

Across the distance, they say memories fade
But all it takes is
One message
One image
One word
One smell
One taste
One ever-elusive touch
And everything returns
To haunt

The there and not-there
The here and not-here
The wanting to be there
and here
Wanting,
Always.

Every night,
Almost every night,
There is this thought.
This hope.
This... feeling —
Tomorrow could be different
Tomorrow, maybe we can be in both places
Tomorrow, maybe we can be both people
Tomorrow, maybe....

Love.
Passion.
Hope.
Guilt.
Rage.
Hate.
Disgust.
Guilt.
Hope.
Guilt.
Hope.
Guilt.
Hope.
Guilt
Hope
Guilt
Hope
Guilt
Hope

> How would you stage this scene?
>
> How many performers would you choose?
>
> What kind of physical location would you set it in?

Do you see me,
like I see you?
Or am I just a periodically emerging mirage
That you call on
Sometimes
That you hope to use
Sometimes
That you love
…
Sometimes.

The I's and the you's and the us's and the them's and the we's and the you's and the
I's —
Possession
Distance
Belonging
Alienation
Always.
The belonging.
And the alienation.

Always distance.
Always possession.

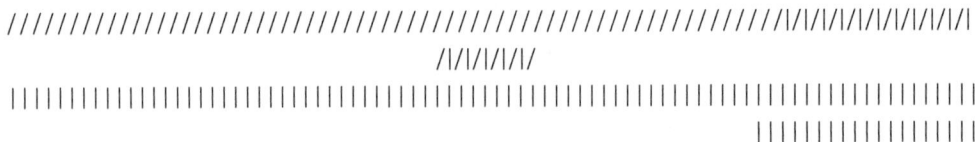

///\/\/\/\/\/\/\/\
/\/\/\/\/\/
||||||||||||||||||||||||||||||||||||||||||||||||||||||||||||||||||||||||||||
|||||||||||||||||

This could be the last time.
And if it were
The last time,
Like the time before was
And the time before that could have been —

This could be the last time.
And if it were,
I think I might break.

Into a million, disconnected pieces.

That could never be whole again.

This could be the last time.

And I wait.

To be broken.

Again.

Whose perspective(s), in your opinion, lie(s) at the heart of this scene?

They say I should write hope
They say I should write difference
They say I should write paths
And options
And ways

And roads
And bridges

But sometimes,
This is all there is to write.

Broken fragments that pour out of you at an airport or train station,
over burnt chai and the never-ending cigarette

Sometimes,
This is all there is.

A deluge.

An outpouring.

A flood.

Across the distance,
I think I see you

Sometimes, I think you see me
But I'm never sure.
I know you aren't either.

We both could go somewhere else.
Be somewhere else.
Choose someone else.
But we keep coming back to each other.
And I have to wonder

Maybe this is not the last time?

• •

The words pour out
Always

The songs torment
Always

We understand.
Sometimes.
Rarely.
Never.
Sometimes

My privilege drowns me
It hurts me

Like a sharp cliché in the middle of my gut.

Do *you* have problems?
Do *you* have worries?

Nothing compared to yours.
But to me,
They become everything
Even when I don't want them to.

This
That
Here
There
You
Me

Binaries.
Always the fucking binaries.

I try
To
Move
Through
Beyond
Above
Below

Sometimes, this is all there is.

Sometimes, this could be the last time.

^^^^^

I want to come to you
To soak in ... everything
To soak in, you
But you and me
We're a binary.
In opposition.
Almost always.

And all that remains

Is this.

Lament.

The wheels, they just keep on turning.

Trrrrrrrrrrrrrrrrrrrrrrrrrrrrrrrrrrrrrrrrrrrrrrrrrrrrrrrrrrrrrrrrrrrrrrrrrrrrrrrrrrrrrrrrrrrrrrrrrrrr
rrrrrrrrrrrrrrrrrrrrrrrrrrrrrrrrrrrrrrrrrrrrrrrrrrrrrrrrrrrrrrrrrrrrrrrrrrrrrrrrrrrrrrrrrrrrrrrrrrrr
rrrrrrrrrrrrrrrrrrrrrrrrrrrrrrrrrrrrrrrrrrrrrrrrrrrrrrrrrrrrrrrrrrrrrrrrrrrrrrrrrrrrrrrrrrrrrrrrrrrr
rrrrrrrrrrrrrrrrrrrrrrrrrrrrrrrrrrrrrrrrrrrrrrrrrrrrrrrrrrrrrrrrrrrrrrrrrrrrrrrrrrrrrrrrrrrrrrrrrrrr
rrrrrrrrrrrrrrrrrrrrrrrrrrrrrrrrrrrrrrrrrrrrrrrrrrrrrrrrrrrrrrrrrrrrrrrrrrrrrrrrrrrrrrrrrrrrrrrrrrrr
　　　　rrrrrrrrrrrrrrrrrrrrrrrrrrrrrrrrrrrrrrrrrrrrrrrrrrrrrrrrrrrrrrrrrrrrrrrrrrrr.

A moment of silence.

The GUIDES lead the audience to the next space down a path made of shards of glass.

The Third Coalition

Like the one that came before, this COALITION is a space of collaborative creation; of a group of people coming together, albeit temporarily, to "make something": an atmosphere, a spirit, a hope, a recognition. As spectators enter this outdoor area, they witness performers sorting trash into specific piles.

Upon arrival, audience members are handed overalls and gloves, and are divided into four groups.

Audience members can choose not to be part of the process. They can choose to simply sit by. But without everyone's participation, won't the composting just take even longer?

The composting is, clearly, an allegory: for taking "trash" and making it something else. For the collective effort it takes. For the proportions that need to be right. For the time it must be given.

And given the directness of the allegory, nothing more has to be said.

Make sure that the audiences are given clear directions on how to compost!

The main composters are actors; Kashmiris. They wear their realities in their bodies; in their breaths. They tell the spectators what to do. They teach them how to compost. And at the very end they say, "Thank you for your help. Now… now only time will tell."

In the middle of the composting process, tea and biscuits are brought in.

Once audience members' groups are done, they are given buckets of water with which to clean their hands. The actors join the audience for tea when their respective groups are finished; the GUIDES indicate that it is time to leave when all the spectator groups are done with their composting tasks.

When leaving this space, the audience walks through a path constructed with sticky mud to get to the next location.

     https://doi.org/10.11647/OBP.0223.23

Scene Thirteen: The Pelters

▶ WATCH THE VIDEO

An outdoor space. A graveyard. Stones. Stones, everywhere. Each PELTER has a stone in their hand.

PELTER #1: Tariq. 12 years old. The coolness of the stones was the only thing that could temper his boiling rage.

PELTER #2: Majid. 25 years old. He wants to inflict pain.

PELTER #3: Shabnam. 33 years old. She is honouring the memory of her husband who was killed three years ago.

PELTER #4: Suhail. 23 years old. He was paid to do this.

PELTER #5: Aadil. 40 years old. He wants the world to know that he is not scared.

PELTER #6: Farooq. 18 years old. He wants to do this because all his friends are doing it.

PELTER #7: Rafiq. 28 years old. He thinks the stones look beautiful as they fly through the air.

PELTER #8: Nafisa. 25 years old. She loves the fact that she is the only unmarried woman in the protest. It makes her feel like a freedom fighter.

> From the PELTERS' individual statements, how would you characterize them, as a group?

PELTER #9: Bashir. 14 years old. He likes the energy of the crowd. He feels stronger like he is part of something much bigger than himself.

PELTER #10: Ghulam Mohammad. I pick up this stone to show the world that even after 70 years, despite the bullets flying from both sides, my spirit remains unbroken. In this war between two giants, it is *our* lives that have been lost. *Our* bones that have

https://doi.org/10.11647/OBP.0223.24

been shattered. *Our* dignity that has been sullied. My struggle will not end till we have our birth right. My struggle will not end till we are liberated from our oppressors. My struggle will not— cannot— end until we are free. And till then, until that day of freedom arrives, this stone will be my weapon.

All the PELTERS take a stone, take aim, and throw it in one direction. They take more stones, throw them in another direction. They scream. They throw stones. There are loud sounds. Smoke. The PELTERS cower in a circle. They console each other. They try to protect each other.

Silence.

GUIDE #1: Is there anything you would like to tell these people?

PELTER #3: What more is there to say?

GUIDE #1: I have a question for you, if I may, *janab*.

PELTER #5: You're Kashmiri?

GUIDE #1: Yes, yes, I am.

PELTER #7: I know what you are going to ask me.

GUIDE #1: You do?

PELTER #1: Yes, I do.

GUIDE #1: So, what's your response?

PELTER #2: (*He smiles*). I know this is not the effective way to protest. I know that stones cannot match the might of guns. I know that the stones are not going to dislodge the mighty oppressors. I know that sometimes, people earn money by throwing these stones.

> PELTER #4 asks actors to place stones on the graves "regardless of what you believe."
>
> What are the complexities of such a position, especially in a conflict zone like Kashmir?

GUIDE #1: So?

PELTER #4: It is the manifestation of anger of the weakest. And at least better than doing nothing to protest.

GUIDE #1: Is it?

PELTER #8: Depends on whom you ask.

PELTER #4: Please. Regardless of what you believe. Help us place these stones on those graves. Let's say a prayer for them.

GUIDE #1 and the PELTERS place the stones on the graves. An Islamic prayer of rest for the dead is chanted.

The actors leave, handing each audience member a stone souvenir that is wrapped with images of children facing/protesting against military tanks and other war paraphernalia (Mary Scully, 2016).

The GUIDES take the audience to the next space down a path made of stones. Lots of stones.

Scene Fourteen: The Banalities

[▶ WATCH THE VIDEO]

In the next space we see SOLDIERS. The SOLDIERS are seated on the floor, leaning against the walls. They watch the audience walk in.
Silence.

SOLDIER #1: You've come too late. You missed all the action.

SOLDIER #2: That's the most action we've seen in months.

GUIDE #2: That's ok. We'll just wait with you.

Long silence. One of the SOLDIERS gets up after a while and walks around. One is playing music on his phone. Another is playing a game. Another is just staring into space. The time taken for this silence should be long enough that the audience experiences the banality of their waiting.

VIDEO #1 plays: a documentary about the lives of Indian Armed Forces soldiers' families. Any documentary that humanizes the soldier. That humanizes his world. A little.

> What are the "banalities" being referred to by the title of this scene?
>
> What effect is created by the intentional weaving in of video material in this scene?

SOLDIER #2: Turn that off. If he comes here now, you're dead.

The SOLDIER who is playing the music turns it off.

Another long silence.

SOLDIER #1: I told you you'd come too late. You missed your chance to see us in action.

GUIDE #1: You were the ones throwing the tear gas at those people near the graveyard?

SOLDIER #2: You saw that?

https://doi.org/10.11647/OBP.0223.25

GUIDE #2: Yes, we were there at the time.

SOLDIER #3: Why were you there?

GUIDE #2: We just wanted to hear their stories.

Pause.

GUIDE #1: You threw a lot of —

SOLDIER #2: Did you see the stones they threw at us?

GUIDE #1: Yes but —

SOLDIER #2: What were we supposed to do?

This scene has made very specific choices about how to dramatize "nothingness" in soldiers' lives.

How would you have chosen to showcase the same theme?

VIDEO #2 plays: a recruitment video that romanticizes the life of a soldier in the Indian Army. SOLDIERS #1, #2, #3 continue with their actions. When VIDEO #2 ends:

Long silence.

GUIDE #2: Have you all been here for a long time?

SOLDIER #3: Feels like years.

GUIDE #2: And how many times have you had to... you know...

SOLDIER #2: Do what we did?

GUIDE #2: Yes.

SOLDIER #1: Too many times. But not often enough.

Pause.

GUIDE #2: So, what do you do when...

SOLDIER #2: When we're not doing what we did?

SOLDIER #1: We wait.

SOLDIER #3: For the other shoe to drop.

SOLDIER #2: For the next stone to be thrown.

SOLDIER #1: And finally, there is something for us to do.

SOLDIER #3: Don't say it like that. It sounds wrong.

SOLDIER #2: It's true though, isn't it?

Pause.

GUIDE #2: I think I should take these people to the next place.

SOLDIER #1: I told you: you've come at the wrong time. Wait, at least take a souvenir with you before you go (*indicating a pile of stone souvenirs covered with the following text*). Let them get something at least.

Months of boredom punctuated by moments of terror

Months of boredom punctuated by moments of terror

Punctuated

Months of boredom punctuated by moments of terror

Months of boredom punctuated by moments of terror

GUIDES lead the audience out of the room to the next space, down a path installed with clocks that tick together and not.

Scene Fifteen: The Time

A room that is full of clocks. Clocks that are hung from the ceiling. Clocks that are nailed on to the walls. Clocks that are placed on tables, chairs, and any other surface. Clocks everywhere. The clocks are all out of sync and tick at different rhythms. The different pacing of the clocks should be obvious enough to be irritating, but not so irritating that it becomes intolerable. It's a fine balance.

The floor is designed to look like a calendar — a calendar with the days of the week written larger than life.

In different parts of the room, there are cages: small cages; big cages. The audience members have to sit in the cages. One of the cages contains a young WOMAN; her cage is a chicken coop. Maybe there's a live chicken in the cage with her. The WOMAN has been living in that cage since she witnessed the murder of her parents many years ago. She greets audience members as they enter. She helps the GUIDE take them to their respective cages. She speaks with them about the sun, the moon, and the stars. She speaks with them about the loss of her parents. Throughout what follows, the WOMAN walks around the audience at her will, entering their cages, playing with them as she sees fit.

A MAN has been seated in the middle of the room. As the audience walks in, he smiles at them — sweetly, sincerely. During each of the sections of text below, MAN has one action: adjusting the clocks. His goal, by the end of the scene, is to get all the clocks to tick together.

The MAN stands on Wednesday. He is himself. He is adjusting the clocks as he speaks.

MAN: I pray.

    I wash myself.

    I ask my father how he slept.

    I thank my wife for breakfast.

    I think about kissing her goodbye.

    I go to work.

    I work.

https://doi.org/10.11647/OBP.0223.26

I work.

I work.

I work.

I work.

I get in the car and drive myself home.

I sit in the traffic and listen to the news.

I think about the world.

I try not to lose hope.

I return from work.

I think about kissing my wife hello.

I thank her for dinner.

I ask my father about his day.

I wash myself.

I pray.

He stops playing with the clocks. He moves back to Wednesday. He performs a ritualized series of actions that reflect the same series in the list above: pray, wash, and so on. The rituals are exact. Specific. Choreographed. He does this for three minutes. Exactly.

MAN goes to Sunday. Sunday is full of bricks. He becomes a woman. The woman adjusts clocks while saying the lines below.

MAN
(as woman): The first thing I do when I wake up, is look at the man who is lying next
    to me. I listen to him breathe. I watch the rise and fall of his chest. Sometimes,
    when I let myself be, I think I can love this man forever. I think that he can know
    me like no other. And then he snores. He snores. And rolls over onto his side.
    Away from me.

What does a philosophical engagement with the notion of time have to do with the experience of conflict (in general) and of Kashmir (specifically)?

Music. The actor stops adjusting the clocks. She moves to the bricks and begins chipping away at them. She is looking for something. For someone. We never know what or who. Just that she is searching for something. The music stops. The remnants of the bricks remain. She does this for three minutes. Approximately.

MAN moves to Friday. He becomes a child. A child who has just finished school for the week. The child skips around the room, adjusting the clocks while he speaks.

MAN
(as child): Today, na... I'm going to go home and play cricket. Papa said that if my team wins, na, he'll bring us back some ice cream. If my team loses... well, he'll still bring us back something. (*He laughs.*) I just hope they don't stop him on the way this time, you know? I love chocolate ice cream. It's my favourite. And if I'm good, papa will get me the chocolate ice cream.

MAN (as child) picks up markers/crayons and begins to decorate Friday with drawings of chocolate ice-cream cones. He draws till the box is full. He takes as long as he needs.

MAN moves to Monday. He walks with a cane.

MAN
(as an older
person): Today I will make it from here to there.

He takes slow steps to a clock and adjusts it.

Today I will try to make it from here to there.

He takes slow steps and stops.

Today I should make it from here to there.

He takes slow steps to a clock and adjusts it.

Today I might make it from here to there.

He takes slow steps and stops.

Today I will get there.

He takes slow steps and stops.

Today I will.

He takes slow steps to a clock and adjusts it.

Maybe today I will.

He takes slow steps back to Monday.

Maybe today I will.

He sits down on Monday.

I will.

He lies down. Places the cane beside him.

He remains laying down for a while. More than three minutes. Less than three minutes. It's up to him.

The clocks have been adjusted. They are all ticking together.

MAN stands up; he is everyone and no one. MAN notices the clocks. He begins to clap/stamp a rhythm that — with the sound of ticking — creates a musicality.

GUIDES (and the audience) begin to keep the rhythm with the actor. When the rhythm has been established, MAN uses the rhythm to jump/hop/dance, between the days that are left. Between Tuesday, Thursday, and Saturday.

Each of these days is filled with a material that is lit on fire. A material that, when lit, emits light and smoke (incense sticks, perhaps? Or pinecones?).

The room is full of smoke. Enough to disorient the spectators a little bit.

As he says the lines below, MAN extinguishes the smoke. Maybe with water. Something else. Something else that adds to the spectators' sensorial experience.

How do you approach time?

How does your community approach time?

If you had to place those approaches to time in conversation with each other — yours and your community's — how would you theatricalize that conversation?

MAN:[1] To some, time is money. Time is a precious, even scarce, commodity. It flows fast, like a mountain river in the spring, and if you want to benefit from its passing, you have to move fast with it. To such people, action is everything. The past is over, but the present you can seize, parcel and package and make it work for you in the immediate future.

Others ignore the passing of time if it means that conversations will be left unfinished. For them, completing a human transaction is the best way they can invest their time. For them, the business they have to do, and their close relations are so important, that it is irrelevant at what time they have to meet. The meeting is what counts.

To some, time is cyclical. Each day the sun rises and sets, the seasons follow one another, the heavenly bodies revolve around us, people grow old and die, but their children reconstitute the process. To such people, when God made time, He made plenty of it.

---

1   (Lewis, 2014)

To the few... time is meaningless.

MAN goes back to Wednesday. He is himself. He is adjusting the clocks as he speaks. This time, the goal is to un-sync them. They begin to tick at a different rhythm again; a different lack of coherence than before.

MAN: I pray.

I wash myself.

My father is dead.

I thank my wife for breakfast.

I can't stand to look at her anymore.

I go to work.

I work.

I work.

I work.

I take the bus home.

I take the bus home so that it takes more time.

I sit in the traffic, hoping the news won't play on the radio.

Again.

There is no point in thinking about the world.

I return from work.

I try to see the beauty in my wife.

I dream about my father.

I wash myself.

I pray.

He stops playing with the clocks. MAN goes to Sunday. Sunday is full of brick pieces. He becomes a woman. The woman adjusts clocks while saying the lines below.

MAN
(as woman): The first thing I do when I wake up, is look for the man who should be lying next to me. I want to listen to him breathe. I want to watch the rise and fall

of his chest. I want to love this man forever. I want him to know me like no other. I want him to snore.

Music. The same music that's slightly different. The actor stops adjusting the clocks. She moves to the bricks and begins trying to put them back together again. She succeeds with some. She throws some away. She stands up. She becomes MAN again.

GUIDE #1 begins to sing a song about time.
He teaches audience members lines of the song.
Call and response.
Everyone sings together.
There is always time to sing.

Except the WOMAN, of course, who remains doing her own thing.
Maybe she joins the chorus.
Maybe she doesn't.

While the song goes on, MAN becomes the child, and then the older person, then back again to being the man and the woman: in three(ish)-minute segments. The character in question gives each audience member a stone souvenir covered with something akin to Trompenaar's model of time perceptions.

At the end of the song, once all audience members have their stone souvenir, MAN goes back to the clocks in the different characters, in three(ish)-minute segments. The WOMAN continues playing with her chickens. The GUIDES take the group to the next space, down a path made of sand.

INSTALLATION D

The general instructions that introduce INSTALLATION A also apply here. The exhibits below are described in no particular order — each one will, ultimately, have to be installed as best fits the chosen site.

Exhibit #1: Activity

A space that is lined with sacks of uncooked rice and demarcated into eight, clearly defined, areas using ropes/tape/wire/something else. Each demarcated area has a number posted in it, and audience members are instructed to place as many grains of rice as the number in that demarcated area.

> The action of counting grains of rice has been used in a variety of art installations and in the training of performance artists.
>
> Engage in the exercise yourself. Count grains of rice for an extended period of time: 30 minutes, for instance.
>
> Consider the effect that this action has on you.

Here, please place the exact number of rice grains as the number posted.

This area has two sections **Section 1: 1500** **Section 2: 4**	**170**	**210**	**7000**

> What makes the act of counting rice poignant in relation to the statistics that are mentioned here?
>
> Or if counting rice doesn't hold significance to you, what action would you replace this with, in the context of this installation?

https://doi.org/10.11647/OBP.0223.27

54	100	**1,25,000** *This space should be set up before the performance, as an example for audience members.*	3

When 20 minutes have passed, the GUIDES place the following signs in each area. Every time this performance is staged, the numbers need to be explicitly attributed to a specific source or to multiple sources.

SIGN	SIGN	SIGN	SIGN
Each grain of rice in this area represents 100 people. Section 1 represents the number of displaced Kashmiri Pandits. Section 2 represents the number of Kashmiri Pandits who have been killed.	Each grain of rice in this area represents 100 people. This area represents the number of civilians killed in Kashmir since 1947.	Each grain of rice in this area represents 100 people. This area symbolizes the number of 'militants' who have been killed in Kashmir since 1947.	Each grain of rice in this area represents 100 people. This area symbolizes the number of government forces who are currently stationed in Kashmir.

SIGN	SIGN	SIGN	SIGN
Each grain of rice in this area represents 100 people. This area symbolizes the number of Indian government forces that have been killed in Kashmir since 1947.	Each grain of rice in this area represents 100 people. This area symbolizes the number of disappearances that have occurred in Kashmir.	Each grain of rice in this area represents 100 people. This area symbolizes the population of Kashmir.	Each grain of rice in this area represents 100 people. This area symbolizes the number of 'militants' who currently operate in Kashmir.

Exhibit #2: Gallery

In a corner, there is a lone woman who is repeating the lines below over and over: lines used in the protests of the Association for the Parents of Disappeared Persons — APDP — in Kashmir.

LADY: Give us — the disappeared children.

Give us — the disappeared husbands.

Give us — the disappeared brothers.

Give us — the disappeared.

LADY is repeating, chanting, these lines at different volumes.

What resonances do you see between APDP and the Madres de la Plaza Mayo in Argentina?

What resonances do you see between stone-pelting as protest in Kashmir and Palestine?

What, if anything, do these transnational connections tell us about the global interconnectedness of protest and oppression?

Exhibit #3: Word Cluster

The following words are displayed, in whatever fashion best fits the space.

Occupied
Controlled
Administered
Autonomous

```
Free
Independent
Overseen
Governed
```

Exhibit #4: Buzzfeed Booth

A poster of the Bollywood film *Jab Jab Phool Khile* is pasted alongside a screening of the same film; the audio comes through speakers and in so doing, becomes the soundscape for the installation space. There should be comfortable seating spaces in front of the screening, allowing spectators to rest and simply watch the video, should they desire to do so.

Suggested Menu for this Installation Space

A rice-based snack, like *phirni*: a dessert that is prepared with rice, milk, a variety of dried fruits, and sugar.

Stone Souvenir

Why broken eggshells?

What effect does the use of this material in the passage between the installation and the following scene create?

During the installation, just as in the preceding scenes, the GUIDES give spectators a souvenir to carry in their bags. Here, the souvenir is a stone that has wrapped around it a piece of paper containing the definition of a "mass grave."

After 30 minutes, the GUIDES lead the spectators out of this space.

As the audience exits this space and moves on to the next one, they walk along a path that is designed using broken eggshells.

Scene Sixteen: The Women

As audience members enter this space, regardless of that person's gender identity, they are asked to dress as Kashmiri women are likely to dress. This is a space that is for women. And if anyone wants to really engage with the stories of Kashmir's women, they need to look for these spaces. They need to make the effort. To understand that feminism in this Valley has its own face. Its own logic. Its own rhythm.

As the spectator-women are seated in the space, they see people behind a screen — as shadows, silhouettes. The shadows are chopping something on wooden blocks. Something that looks like hair. The hair-chopping shadows provide the rhythm for what follows. The action and sound continue throughout the scene.

Look into the lives of the women who are the protagonists of this scene: Atiqa Banoo, Nighat Sahiba, Lal Ded, Habba Khatoon, and Parveena Ahangar.

Consider these women's significance in Kashmiri history and, consequently, the significance of their inclusion in *Chronicles from Kashmir.*

There are five women in front of the screen: Atiqa Banoo (AB); Nighat Sahiba (NS); Lal Ded (LD); Habba Khatoon (HK); Parveena Ahangar (PA). AB is building something… using stones, perhaps. Each stone has, written on it, names of particular aspects of Kashmiri culture and heritage that AB fought to preserve: the language; the customs; the particularities of the Valley's inhabitants.

While NS, LD, and HK speak, PA is making flyers for the disappeared — the same flyers (and actor) should be used outside Installation D; they are also the flyers that cover the stone souvenirs that are handed to audience members during the scene below; the same stones that AB is also using. Some audience members can be invited to make the flyers and stone souvenirs with PA.

At some point in what follows, AB and PA hand out stone souvenirs to each spectator.

Other audience members, in their roles as women, are given a host of different tasks to take on — by the GUIDES, or by PA and AB:

- *One person is asked to iron clothing*
- *One person is asked to peel potatoes*

    https://doi.org/10.11647/OBP.0223.28

- *One person is seated by a small stove and is provided with materials to make chai*
- *One person is given a toy gun*
- *One person is given paper and pens*
- *One person is given photos of men, with a marker*

You get the picture.

The woman reciting the poems below can move around the space. They can be more formally "staged." Whatever works.

LD:[1] To learn the scriptures is easy, to live them, hard. The search for the Real is no simple matter.

HK:[2] Which rival of mine has lured you away from me? Why are you cross with me? Forget the anger and the sulkiness, You are my only love, Why are you cross with me? My garden has blossomed into colourful flowers, Why are you away from me?

NS:[3] Either you will succumb or rise. I chose to rise.

I collected my scattered parts to rise.

Nobody fights for us.

Nobody fought for me.

You have to fight your own battle

Yes, I am a feminist.

HK: Which rival of mine has lured you away from me? Why are you cross with me? Forget the anger and the sulkiness, You are my only love, Why are you cross with me? My garden has blossomed into colourful flowers, Why are you away from me?

NS: *Daed balnas chu akh zamane lagan*

Daagh tschalnas chu akh zamane lagan

Yei zi pahra agar mokul aasakh

Posh pholnas chu akh bahane lagan

LD: Deep in my looking, the last words vanished. Joyous and silent, the waking that met me there.

---

1   (Ded, n.d.)
2   (Khatoon, n.d.)
3   (Geelani, 2017)

HK: My love, my only love, I think only of you, Why are you cross with me? I kept my doors open half the night, Come and enter my door, my jewel, Why have you forsaken the path to my house? Why are you cross with me? I swear, my love, I am waiting for you, dressed in colourful robes, My youth is in full bloom now, Why are you cross with me?

NS: I kill myself

in saving every minute item that I possess.

In my strife in saving

I scream out:

HK: Oh, marksman, my bosom is open To the darts you throw at me. These darts are piercing me, Why are you cross with me? I have been wasting away like snow in summer heat. My youth is in its bloom. This is your garden, come and enjoy it. Why are you cross with me?

NS: For the pain to heal,

eons it does take

For the scars to fade

eons it does take

Come, for a moment,

If a moment you possess

For the buds to bloom,

a moment it does take

HK: I have sought you over hills and dales, I have sought you from dawn till dusk, I have cooked dainty dishes for you. I do all this in vain! Why are you cross with me? I shed incessant tears for you, I am pining for you, What is my fault, O, my love? Why don't you seek me out? Why are you cross with me?

LD: Some, who have closed their eyes, are wide awake. Some, who look out at the world, are fast asleep. Some who bathe in sacred pools remain dirty. Some are at home in the world but keep their hands clean.

HK: The shock of your desertion has come as a blow to me, O cruel one, I continue to nurse the pain. Why are you cross with me? I have not complained even to the spring breeze That is my agony. Why have you forgotten me? Who will take care of me? Why are you cross with me? I swear by you I do not go out at all, I don't even show up at the spring. My body is burning, Why don't you soothe it? Why are you cross with me? My hurt is marrow deep; I did not complain. I just wasted away for you. I have suppressed endless longing, Why are you cross with me?

NS: O you, who are dying, take me along!

HK: I, Habba Khatun, am grieving now.

LD: What the books taught me, I've practised. HK: Why didn't I ever greet you, my love?

LD: What they didn't teach me, I've taught myself.

NS: O you, who are living, keep me held tight.

HK: The day is fading, and I keep recalling,

NS: Either you will succumb or rise. I chose to rise.

LD: I've gone into the forest and wrestled with the lion.

NS: I collected my scattered parts to rise.	HK: Why are you cross with me?	LD: I didn't get this far by teaching one thing and doing another.

What is the significance of the imagery of the hair-choppers and the hair chopping?

All five women walk behind the screen, where the hair chopping has continued the entire time.

There is a choreographed sequence with the shadows. Sometimes, the women seem to have the power; at other times, the hair-choppers do.

After a few iterations of this choreography, the GUIDES indicate to the audience to follow them and walk the group to the next space, down a path made of mirrors.

Scene Seventeen: The Game Show

WATCH THE VIDEO

The space is set up like a game show.

HOST: *Namaskar, namaskar, namaskar*! Welcome to *Kaun Banega Crorepati*. Today we have three participants in our show and the prize money will go to the person who knows the most about Kashmir! Contestants, please introduce yourselves.

> *Namaskar*
> Greetings
>
> *Kaun Banega Crorepati*
> Who wants to be a millionaire?

GUEST #1: Hello everyone. While I've never been to Kashmir before, I have been studying a lot about its history and current affairs. By winning this prize money, I want to apply for an MA in Political Science.

GUEST #2: Good morning. Like my friend, I too have never been to Kashmir and if I win this money, I would like to take my first trip there!

GUEST #3: Hi everyone. I come from very far away and I am here to learn more about Kashmir as much as to share my knowledge. If I win this money, I will... I don't know yet what I will do (*laughs*).

HOST: Excellent. Now that you've introduced yourselves, let me quickly explain the rules of the game. As you know, you will be asked a series of questions, and, starting with Rs. 1000, for every correct answer, you can win greater and greater sums of money. When a question is asked, the first person to ring the buzzer in front of them will get to respond first. If they answer correctly, that person will be asked another question to double their winnings. If they answer incorrectly, I will provide the correct answer and move on to the next question. If you ever do not know the answer to a question, each of you can use our three lifelines: Audience Poll, Fifty-Fifty and Phone-A-Friend. Ready? Ladies and gentlemen. Our first question:

https://doi.org/10.11647/OBP.0223.29

what is the capital of Pakistan-Administered Kashmir or Azad Kashmir, as it is also known?

a) Srinagar

b) Islamabad

c) Muzaffarabad

d) Lahore

GUEST #1 presses the buzzer.

GUEST #1: Islamabad!

HOST: The correct answer is Muzzafarabad. OK, let's move on to the second question. Where is Kargil?

a) Jammu

b) Pakistan

c) Ladakh

d) Kashmir

GUEST #3 presses the buzzer.

GUEST#3: Ladakh

HOST: Correct! You have won 1,000 rupees! Let's hear some applause for this contestant, ladies and gentlemen.

Audience applauds (led by the GUIDES).

HOST: Now to our second question for this contestant. If he answers this one correctly also, he can double his winnings to 2000 Rupees. What is at the heart of the conflicts in Kashmir? The options are:

a) A desire for self-determination

b) Conflicts between India and Pakistan

c) Terrorists

d) None of the above

GUEST #3: Can I have a lifeline please, sir?

HOST: Sure, which one would you like to use?

GUEST #3: Can we have the audience poll please?

HOST: Of course, audience, please help our guest win 2000 Rs. Here is the question again: What is at the heart of the Kashmir issue? The options are:

a) A desire for self-determination

b) Conflicts between India and Pakistan

c) Terrorists

d) None of the above

Who says option a); please raise your hands. Option b)? Option c)? Option d)?

HOST counts the responses and announces what the audience poll suggests. Regardless of the answer given by the audience:

GUEST #3: I'm going to say that the answer is b): conflicts between India and Pakistan.

HOST: That answer is... incorrect! The correct answer was a): a desire for self-determination. You, sir, remain at 1,000 Rs. Next question for all the contestants. Where are Gilgit and Baltistan located?

a) Jammu

b) Kashmir

c) Pakistan

d) Ladakh

GUEST #2 presses the buzzer.

GUEST #2: Ladakh!

HOST: Incorrect. The correct answer is... anyone in the audience?

Audience is given a chance to answer.

HOST: The correct answer is c): Gilgit and Baltistan are administered by Pakistan. All right, let's make this more exciting now. The next question is a bonus question and whoever gets this right will get 10,000 Rs! Ready? Ok. For a prize of 10,000 Rs the question is: What does AFSPA stand for?

a) Armed Forces Special Powers Act

b) Act for Soldiers' Protection and Autonomy

c) All Friends of Pakistan and America

> If you had to design a
> game show that asked
> contestants to showcase
> their knowledge about
> income inequality in your
> community, what would
> the rules of that game
> be?
>
> What kinds of questions
> would you ask?
>
> Who would be your ideal
> contestant pool?

None of the above

GUEST #3 presses the buzzer.

GUEST #3: a) Armed Forces Special Powers Act.

HOST: YES! Correct. Congratulations. You have now won 10,000 Rs in addition to your existing 1,000 Rs prize. You are now leading with 11,000 Rs. Sir, you have a great opportunity now. If you answer this follow up bonus question correctly, you can now double your winnings to 22,000 Rs immediately. Are you ready?

GUEST #3: Yes, sir!

HOST: The question for 22,000 Rs is: What is the most feasible solution to Kashmir's conflicts?

a) Create more ways for Kashmiris to identify with India

b) Search for a political solution that involves discussions with Kashmir, India, and Pakistan

c) Increase tourism to Kashmir

d) None of the above

Pause.

GUEST #3: Could I have another lifeline, sir? I would like to call a friend.

HOST: Of course. And who will you be calling today?

GUEST #3: My father, sir.

HOST: OK.

Sounds of a phone call being made.

VOICE: Hello?

GUEST #3: Papa it's me. I'm calling from *Kaun Banega Crorepati* and I need your help.

VOICE: Of course, of course. Hello everyone!

HOST: Hello, sir. Thank you for helping your son today!

VOICE: Of course, sir. I'm a big fan of the show. What is the question?

GUEST #3: Dad, the question is: What is the most feasible solution to Kashmir's conflicts?

a) Create more ways for Kashmiris to identify with India

b) Search for a political solution that involves discussions with Kashmir, India, and Pakistan

c) Increase tourism to Kashmir

d) None of the above

HOST: Can you help your son, sir?

VOICE: Yes. I think so. Let me see... I think the answer is definitely a). We must create more ways for Kashmiris to identify with India. Yes, that's the most feasible solution.

HOST: Thank you very much, sir. We appreciate your help.

VOICE: Yes, yes. Thank you. Good luck, *beta*! The answer is a).

Sound of phone call ending.

HOST: So, sir. For the question about the most feasible solution to Kashmir's crises, what is your answer? Are you going to go with your father's answer or choose something else?

Pause.

HOST: You have fifteen seconds left to make your decision.

GUEST #3: Sir... I'm not sure but I think I will agree with my father and choose a).

HOST: Our guest chooses option a): that what is needed is to create more ways for Kashmiris to identify with being Indian. That is... INCORRECT, ladies and gentlemen. The right answer is b), the search for a political solution.

GUEST #2: Wait, what?

HOST: That is the right answer sir.

GUEST #2: According to whom? That's not right. Option b) is not the right answer. Option a) is the correct answer.

HOST: Unfortunately —

GUEST #1: Please stop using this show for your own propaganda sir. Kashmir is an integral part of India — all we need to do is build more healthy relationships between people.

GUEST #2: Yes. Leave all this self-determination stuff aside and just focus on what's real.

HOST: This is not a political de —

GUEST #1: This is political as soon as you ask about a solution to what is happening in Kashmir.

GUEST #2: Yes, do not run away from the issue.

HOST: Look sirs, you need to calm —

GUEST #1: I find all your questions to be offensive and seditious. You know I could report you for this?

HOST: No, sir. No need to do that… We just have to…

GUEST #2: What kind of political quiz show is this? This is nonsense. Please stop spreading your own agenda around

GUEST #1: That's right.

GUEST #3: Come on, folks. We're on television. They've created the questions —

GUEST #2: I don't care. You can't just provide wrong answers like this.

> Consider a historical event that you have studied.
>
> Rewrite that event's history by using a perspective that was not included in your study of that event.

GUESTS #1, #2 & #3 start arguing. HOST beckons security guards who come and drag the GUESTS outside. The title song plays loudly to drown the fighting.

HOST: Thank you all for coming. Good night.

HOST exits.

GUIDE #2: Sorry about that, ladies and gentlemen. Everyone has an opinion about Kashmir… I would like to ask you all a question. So much of what people think they know about Kashmir is based on what they have been taught in school.

I looked at the history and politics textbooks from (*insert name of place in which performance is being conducted and use textbooks that are specific to that context*) and I was surprised to see what they actually include about Kashmir (*make reference to chapter names; number of pages; whatever is relevant in that book*). Imagine that you have the power to design a textbook that would include a section about Kashmir — what would you want it to contain?

GUIDE #1: You will see blank sheets of paper in the different corners of this room, and next to them, you have been provided materials to write with. We welcome you to design your own textbook — what would your book contain? You can use these existing textbooks for your reference.

The HOST and the GUIDES facilitate the division of the spectators into groups. Each group is given some time to design a textbook about Kashmir — with topic headings of what such a schoolbook should include. Once all groups are done with their creations, the GUIDES encourage the groups to walk around and see each other's work.

When done, the GUIDES take the spectators to the next space along a path created using strobe lighting. Maybe the audience members are blindfolded as they go down this path?

INSTALLATION E

The general instructions that introduce INSTALLATION A also apply here. The exhibits below are described in no particular order — each one will, ultimately, have to be installed as best fits the chosen site.

Exhibit #1: Gallery

An asylum. In different corners of the room, simultaneous acts are happening.

In front of each PERSON, below, there is a pad that is hanging from the ceiling. The kind of pad on which doctor's notes are written. There is a pen near each pad. The pad has two columns: "Diagnosis" & "Treatment." There are examples of answers already written on these notes by actors. Audience members can choose to write their responses on the pads.

PERSON #1 is obsessively cleaning the space around her. She dusts, sweeps, and then cleans the floor with phenyl. Every time it seems like she is almost done, she finds another spot to scrub. Something else to put in order.

PERSON #2 is staring into a mirror, talking to himself. He keeps telling himself esteem-building statements: "You are handsome," "You are intelligent," "You are talented."

PERSON #3 is sitting on the floor, staring in front of himself. He is unable to do anything. He looks at the window and it seems like he wants to look outside, but he loses interest. He tries to read a book and again it looks like he is going to read it, but he loses interest.

PERSON #4 can only stare out of the window. He bites his nails. He paces. He's waiting for the next teargas shell to be dropped. For the next protest to arise. At any slightly loud sound he jumps in fright.

PERSON #5 has had surgery of some sort. He is lying on the floor with bandages around his head and stomach.

PERSON #6 is playing with words; words from this sentence: "I may not agree with what you say, but I shall defend to my death your right to say it" that have been cut into individual pieces. Each word from the sentence is written on an individual piece of paper/cardboard. Think of it as a huge jigsaw puzzle.

https://doi.org/10.11647/OBP.0223.30

PERSON #6: I may not agree with what you say, but I shall defend to my death your right to say it.

S/he looks at an imaginary person who is giving feedback.

PERSON #6: Right. Yes, yes of course. I see your point. I'll change it.

S/he rearranges the words again.

PERSON #6: I shall defend your right.

S/he looks at an imaginary person who is giving feedback.

PERSON #6: No but that's not what I — but you see, the thing that I want to — but PLEASE —

S/he looks down, dejected, and rearranges the words again.

PERSON #6: My death shall not agree with you.

S/he looks at an imaginary person who is giving feedback.

PERSON #6: Look. These are my words. Our words. We can do with them as we wish... What do you mean? No. You cannot do that. No you cannot do that. I will complain. I will... You cannot do that to me.

S/he looks down, angry, and rearranges in anger.

PERSON #6: I defend my right.

S/he looks at an imaginary person who is giving feedback.

PERSON #6: Sir please — please — no, I'm sorry. Please don't do that. Please. I really need this and... I'm sorry. I'm so sorry. It won't happen again. What do you want me to say? Fine. Fine, I'll say that.

S/he rearranges the words again.

PERSON #6: I agree with you.

S/he looks at an imaginary person who is giving feedback.

PERSON #6: I'm glad you like it.

Silence.

The ACTOR stares at the last line that has been created "I agree with you." S/he makes as many of these sentences as possible using the words that are lying on the floor. Each time she assembles the sentence, her emotions shift. Sometimes she is upset. At other times she is emotionless and numb. The room is eventually covered with "I agree with you."

Exhibit #2: Word Cluster

The following words are displayed, in whatever fashion best fits the space.

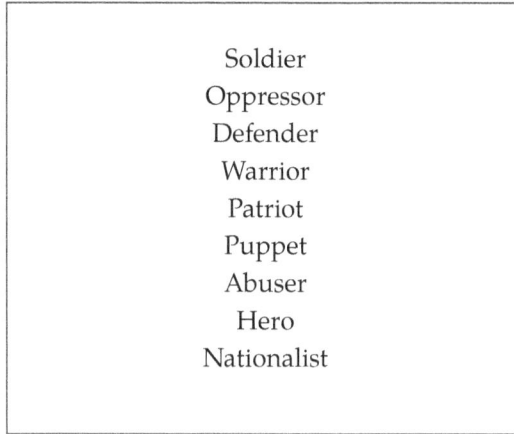

Soldier
Oppressor
Defender
Warrior
Patriot
Puppet
Abuser
Hero
Nationalist

Exhibit #3: Activity

An actor, playing a DOCTOR, sits at a table near which the sign below is placed.

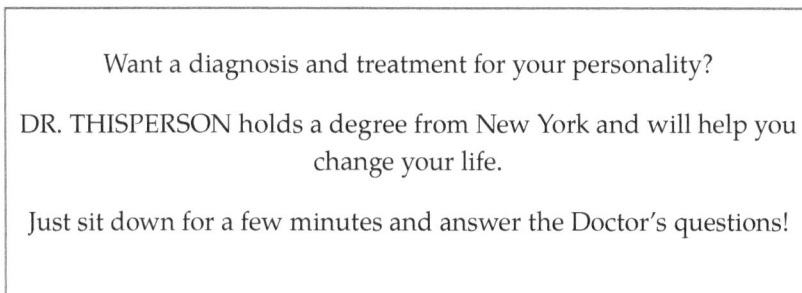

Want a diagnosis and treatment for your personality?

DR. THISPERSON holds a degree from New York and will help you change your life.

Just sit down for a few minutes and answer the Doctor's questions!

As audience members come for their diagnoses, the doctor speaks with them: asking questions about themselves — not too personal, but personal enough. He then uses their responses to form a diagnosis. Not of any "real" illness. But of something that captures an existential affliction, for which the DOCTOR suggests an inane treatment plan. Possible diagnoses and treatment ideas are listed below.

Possible Diagnoses	Possible Treatments
Shows a high risk of potentially finding evolution to be an insufficient explanation for life on earth	Needs to consume more carrots
Shows a medium risk of being confused by the purpose of life	Needs to make 1,000 more Facebook friends
Shows a low risk of seeing the world in hues of purple	Needs to make contact with the doctor who delivered them
Shows a high risk for being confounded by human proclivity for war	Needs to achieve world peace
Seems conflicted about the existence of God	Recommend that the patient reads the holy books of all great world religions

Exhibit #4: Buzzfeed Booth

A poster of the film *BSF: India's First Line of Defence* is pasted alongside a screening of the same film; the audio comes through speakers and in so doing, becomes the soundscape for the installation space. There should be comfortable seating spaces in front of the screening, allowing spectators to rest and simply watch the video, should they desire to do so.

Suggested Menu for this Installation Space

Snacks and drinks that look like they could be medicine: think of pill-shaped candy; drinks that have the consistency of antacid.

Stone Souvenir

During the installation, just as in the preceding scenes, the GUIDES give spectators a souvenir to carry in their bags. Here, the souvenir is a stone that has wrapped around it a piece of paper containing text about the intersections between mental health and war, especially in Kashmir. Consider the following resources: Murthy & Lakshminarayana (2006) and Tamim (2016).

After 30 minutes, the GUIDES ask the audience to follow them to the next location.

As the audience exits this space, they are invited to wear blindfolds for their walk to the next location. If they are not comfortable wearing blindfolds, they are asked to close their eyes. If they are not comfortable doing that either, well, it's their journey.

Scene Eighteen: The Hideout

⊙ WATCH THE VIDEO

A room that is lined with leaves. Dry leaves. Wet leaves. Branches. Creepers. The room should be designed to look like a forest. The GUIDES stop right outside the door to the room.

GUIDE #2: As important as the stories that are heard, are the voices that remain silent. Some because they choose not to speak. Others because they are told not to speak. Yet others who cannot speak. In this room, I want to share with you a silence that I have encountered. A narrative that I have not been able to get near, as a non-Kashmiri. In the room that we are about to enter I invite you to reflect, with me, upon this silence. Please take off your blindfolds now but keep them with you!

The group enters the room and any conversation that occurs between the GUIDES takes place in whispers and hushed voices. There is a soundscape of a forest: silence, punctuated with the rustling of leaves, the breaking of branches, the sound of crickets. GUIDE #2 flinches at every sound, looking as though he is expecting someone to come. After five minutes of this silent waiting have passed:

GUIDE #1: Are we expecting someone?

GUIDE #2: I was told that a meeting might be possible and to wait here with the group at this precise hour.

A few seconds of silence.

GUIDE #1: They knew you were bringing a group?

GUIDE #2: Yes.

GUIDE #1: And they agreed to the meeting?

GUIDE #2: Well, they didn't so much agree as indicate that maybe they would be here at the same time.

   https://doi.org/10.11647/OBP.0223.31

A few seconds of silence.

GUIDE #1: You know they probably think that you have an agenda?

GUIDE #2: Yes. But most Kashmiris think that I have an agenda. Nothing different about these guys.

GUIDE #1: Nothing but the fact that they have weapons.

GUIDE #2 goes over to GUIDE #1 and whispers, vehemently, that the latter refrain from saying things that will scare the audience members.

Five more minutes of silent waiting. The soundscape evolves. From only forest sounds and sounds of rustling leaves, we hear indistinguishable voices in the distance.

GUIDE #2: Let's give them five more minutes, ok?

Asalaam alaikum
May peace be upon you

Walaikum asalaam
And may peace be upon you as well
(a common greeting in Islamic cultures and communities)

A WOMAN walks in. The WOMAN never looks at GUIDE #2. All her questions and all her comments are directed at GUIDE #1.

GUIDE #1: *Asalaam alaikum.*

WOMAN: *Walaikum asalaam.* What are you people doing here?

GUIDE #2: We're just waiting for our friends to arrive and meet us here.

WOMAN: You have friends coming here?

GUIDE #2: Yes.

WOMAN: I think I know your friends.

GUIDE #2: I'm sorry? I don't understand how you... Oh. Right. You know my friends.

Who are the "friends" that are being referred to in the scene?

Why is there so much ambiguity around who is awaited?

Who does the WOMAN represent?

WOMAN: They will not be coming today.

GUIDE #2: Why not?

WOMAN: I don't think you are in any position to ask that question.

GUIDE #2: Sorry. That's not what I meant...

GUIDE #1: I'm sorry, madam. We were just excited to meet them. That's all my friend meant.

WOMAN: Well, they will not be coming today so you better get going.

GUIDE #2: Perhaps you could talk to us?

WOMAN: About what?

GUIDE #2: About your friends.

WOMAN: What do you want to know?

GUIDE #1: Whatever you are willing to share.

Pause. The WOMAN looks around the room carefully.

WOMAN: Where are these people from?

GUIDE #1: From outside Kashmir.

WOMAN: Why are they here?

GUIDE #1: They want to learn more about Kashmir.

WOMAN: I don't have the time to teach them.

Silence. WOMAN looks at different people in the room. She picks audience members at random and asks them where they are from and what they want to learn about Kashmir. Audience members can answer or not, as they wish. In either case the WOMAN looks at each of them in an intimidating fashion. She questions each and every person in the room, ending with GUIDE #1.

WOMAN: This was your idea, correct?

GUIDE #1: No —

GUIDE #2: No, madam, it was mine.

WOMAN: Idiot. Don't you realize how much danger you have put these people and your friends in by coming here?

GUIDE #1 looks down, ashamed at being disrespected in front of his guests. GUIDE #2 tries to interrupt the WOMAN and tell her that it was his decision to bring the group to the rebels' hideout, but she doesn't even look at him. GUIDE #2 is upset, guilty that his comrade has to bear the brunt of the WOMAN's wrath for something that is GUIDE #2's doing.

GUIDE #2: I... umm... they said...

WOMAN: I don't know who told you what but coming here with all these people was a stupid thing to do. You're Kashmiri. Shouldn't you know better than this? What is wrong with you? Forgetting your roots to endear yourself to strangers? You should be ashamed of yourself. You better leave.

The WOMAN goes on her way, exiting in a different direction from which she entered. Silence.

GUIDE #1 seems paralyzed, with fear and shame. He moves away from GUIDE #2. GUIDE #2 looks at his comrade for a few seconds and then moves over to him.

GUIDE #2: Sir, I'm so sorry — Sir, they told me they would be here, and I assumed —

> *Pangas*
> Colloquial term to refer to picking fights

GUIDE #1: You assumed? You thought you could have the privilege of assuming things with people who have weapons?... You keep talking as if you understand Kashmir so well. Kashmir this, Kashmir that. How much do you understand if you don't know this? You cannot take *pangas* with these people...

GUIDE #2: Sir —

GUIDE #1: Sir, nothing. You'll do this trip and you'll leave. I'm the one who has to stay here. I'm the one who has to live with the consequences of this... You need to apologize to all these people here. Do you know the danger you've put them in?

> What is the significance of showing GUIDE #2's breakdown?

GUIDE #2 looks around the audience and goes to each one. "I'm so sorry," he says to each one. Apologizing. Crying. Regretting. He ends his round of apologies in front of GUIDE #1. He is unable to look at him.

Silence.

GUIDE #2: I think we should cancel the rest of the programme, sir.

GUIDE #1: What?

GUIDE #2: You're right. I don't understand as much as I thought... I put these people at risk. I've upset you. I... I think it'll be better for everyone if we cancel the rest of the programme.

GUIDE #1: No. Absolutely not. We have guests here. We can't just cancel things.

GUIDE #2: But sir, why will any of them want to follow me after this?

GUIDE #1: I think they will understand that we all make mistakes. It will be worse for us to cancel now and leave things like this...

Pause.

GUIDE #2: And you and me? Are we ok?

GUIDE #1: We will be.

GUIDE #2 slowly turns to the audience.

GUIDE #2: Ladies and gentlemen, I apologize for this. I didn't think this through properly. I hope you will still come with me on what's left of the journey... All I can tell you is that.... Things like this happen more often than you'd think. Every time I come here, I realize... however much one learns about Kashmir... it's never enough.

Please put your blindfolds back on.

The audience is led to the next space.

Scene Nineteen: The Return

▶ WATCH THE VIDEO

Split scene. Three pairs of actors. Each pair has two characters: one Kashmiri Muslim and one Kashmiri Pandit. The pairs are staged at different locations on the periphery of the space, with the audience seated in the middle. In each pair the two men/women are childhood friends who are reconnecting after a long time. When the audience enters, each pair is frozen in a different tableau. One pair is hugging and crying. One pair is sitting across a table from each other. One pair has their backs to each other.

PANDIT #3: I miss Kashmir.

MUSLIM #3: Why don't you come back?

PANDIT #3: *Dil toh chahta hai* but people keep talking about the *"halaat"*...

MUSLIM #3: What about the *halaat*?

PANDIT #3: I hear every day that things in Kashmir are not good. That there are still... well, you know what I mean.

> *Dil toh chahta hai*
> The heart wants it
>
> *Halaat*
> The condition/the situation

Change in focus.

MUSLIM #2: Look, I'm not going to lie and tell you that everything is fine. But you should know that whatever the h*alaat* is going to be for you, that's how it's going to be for me also. If they try to hurt you, it'll be over my dead body.

PANDIT #2: That is really sweet of you to say. But how can Kashmir be my home again if I have to rely on you or stay in a camp to be safe?

MUSLIM #2: That's not what I'm saying. I'm saying that if things remain unsafe for you... I was a child last time and I couldn't help. But this time, I can do something.

 https://doi.org/10.11647/OBP.0223.32

The safest place for Pandits will be in the hearts of Kashmiri Muslims — not in the camps.

Pause.

PANDIT #2: Some of our people are telling us that we should not go on an individual basis until there is a plan for how to settle the entire community. Others are telling us that we should start going back and test how things are. Others are talking about creating demarcated areas in which we can live under some kind of protection. And some, some even want a part of Kashmir just for our community. I don't know whom to believe any more.

MUSLIM #2: Whom do you want to believe?

PANDIT #2: The dreamer in me — the part of me who will always consider Kashmir my home — wants to listen to those who tell me that I can go back without fear. But the realist in me — the part of me who remembers what made me leave...

MUSLIM #2: That part of you doesn't know what to do.

PANDIT #2: Yes... If we return, will we get our jobs back?

MUSLIM #2: I'm sure they are looking to put some sort of plan in place.

PANDIT #2: But what about the unemployed Kashmiri youth? Won't our return add to the pressure of the jobs that already need to be created? Won't that create more resentment towards us?

MUSLIM #2: That's a good question... and we also need the jobs. I don't know the answer to that question.

Change in focus.

PANDIT #1: What about our homes?

MUSLIM #1: Would you consider selling your current home and using that money to build a new home in Kashmir?

PANDIT #1: Should I?

MUSLIM #1: Why not?

PANDIT #1: What if it all happens again?

Pause.

MUSLIM #1: You won't know till you take the chance.

PANDIT #1: Easy for you to say. You're not the one who has to risk his life.

MUSLIM #1: Kashmiris have to risk their lives every day!

PANDIT #1: Oh, come on. Don't make this a competition about who has suffered more. We have all suffered. The difference is, no one forced you to leave your home.

MUSLIM #1: No one forced you to leave your home either. Look at the Sikhs — they stayed.

Change in focus.

PANDIT #3: There we go again. "Why did those Pandits have to leave? They could have stayed." Let's see if you say the same thing when the men with guns come knocking on your door.

MUSLIM #3: They have come, many times. I didn't leave.

PANDIT #3: It's not the same thing.

MUSLIM #3: Stop making excuses. Why don't you just tell the truth?

PANDIT #3: And what is the truth according to you?

MUSLIM #3: You don't want to come back because then, all this attention you are getting for your story will go away.

PANDIT #3: How dare you say that!

MUSLIM #3 and PANDIT #3 get into a fight with each other. Punches are thrown and they are on rolling around on the floor. Suddenly PANDIT #3 starts laughing uncontrollably:

PANDIT #3: Don't punch me there, please, it tickles.

MUSLIM #3: I guess some things don't change.

Both men collapse in laughter.

As pair #3 is laughing, pairs #1 and #2 pick up balls of wool, and by looping the wool around different parts of the space and audience members' bodies/spaces between them, create a web. The following conversations, then, happen while the six actors are creating this huge web between the bodies and the space. The speed of the conversation increases, as does its intensity. It should be unclear, at the end, who is responding to whom.

> What is the significance of the audience building a web with the actors?

MUSLIM #1: I'll give you my land. Build a house there.

PANDIT #3: What?

MUSLIM #2: I'm serious.

PANDIT #2: They'll never allow this to happen. They're going to paint me as a betrayer to the cause.

MUSLIM #3: So, what? Let them say what they want to say. What's more important? Coming home or...

PANDIT #1: Or my relationship with my community? Both are important.

PANDIT #2: Look, this issue of us returning has to be addressed at a policy level. Individual cases of Muslims hosting Pandits till they feel safe is not only ridiculous, it's useless.

MUSLIM #1: OK. But what about policies to ensure that with the Pandits' return, Muslims who have had to take over their jobs and buy their homes are not suddenly left without employment or houses?

PANDIT #1: So, you agree that policy changes are what's needed at this point? Can you ensure that your fellow Muslims don't invite Pandits to come back on a one-to-one basis and then mediatize these invitations as "proof" of things being better?

MUSLIM #3: I can try my best to ensure that we get enough people behind us, but I cannot ensure that people will not invite their friends back on a one-to-one basis. This is a free country, after all!

> Each different conversation between a MUSLIM and PANDIT pair showcases a different dimension to the historical narratives of conflict and reconciliation between these communities.
>
> What are these different dimensions?
>
> What are the dimensions to the Kashmiri Muslim-Pandit that are still absent from this scene?

PANDIT #2: Is it?

Change in focus.

MUSLIM #1: Maybe it's better for you to be careful. Don't come back till you're sure that you will be safe.

PANDIT #2: I want to come home. But I can't.

MUSLIM #3: I am with you. They'll have to kill me before they can get to you.

PANDIT #2: I don't want anything to do with Kashmir anymore.

MUSLIM #1: You should only come back if you're ready to start from scratch again.

PANDIT #2: They should give us our own space; our own little slice of Kashmir.

MUSLIM #2: Come back only if you can be part of our struggle.

PANDIT #1: I'll only return if I can get my house and my job back.

MUSLIM #3: I really want you to come back but... not everyone feels that way.

PANDIT #2: Promise me that we'll be safe.

PANDIT #3: No.

MUSLIM #1: Yes.

MUSLIM #2: Maybe.

PANDIT #1: Should I?

MUSLIM #2: Shouldn't?

PANDIT #3: Can I?

MUSLIM #1: Why?

PANDIT #2: Why not?

PANDIT #1: When?

MUSLIM #3: How?

PANDIT #2: May I?

MUSLIM #2: Yes.

MUSLIM #1: No.

PANDIT #3: Maybe.

MUSLIM #3: Why?

PANDIT #1: May I?

MUSLIM #2: Why not?

The repetition of these words gets faster and faster until they reach a crescendo. GUIDE #2's irritation has only been growing, as he gets enmeshed within the web.

GUIDE #2: STOP.

All the MUSLIMS and PANDITS freeze.

GUIDE #2: What would you like us to do?

ALL ACTORS
(MUSLIMS & PANDITS): Find a way out.

The way in which the web is wound should not make it too easy for the audience members to disentangle themselves from it. GUIDE #1 is the first to extricate himself and he helps each spectator free themselves from the web. Once GUIDE #2 is free, he starts handing stone souvenirs to audience members who are free of the web. Each stone is covered, simply, with the following terms:

Repatriation
Reintegration
Rehabilitation
Reconstruction

The group moves to the next space, navigating a webbed pathway.

Scene Twenty: The Seesaws

A room full of seesaws. Audience sits on seesaws.

The characters speaking these lines are also on seesaws. The characters are in fatigues: they could be representatives of a nation-state's armed forces, or a group of guerrillas.

There is a rhythm playing in the background. Everyone must COLLECTIVELY move the seesaws in sync, according to the rhythm. If anyone goes off the rhythm — at any time — the lighting changes; a siren plays for 15 seconds. Back to the rhythm and the seesaws.

Ideally, the rules of this world are communicated to audience members non-verbally, after a few times of them going off rhythm when they first start on the seesaws, only to be met with changing lights and the sounds of sirens — the audience should be taught the rules of the world in this way.

> What is the significance of the seesaws and the changing rhythms in which they move?
>
> Who are the different identity groups that the PERSONS IN FATIGUES might represent?

The sound and lighting operator control the scene, essentially. They watch for people going off rhythm. They cause the scene to start and stop. The actors need to pick from where they left off. As if nothing happened. And yet, knowing something has.

PERSON IN
FATIGUES #1: A bit of shame. That's a lie, there's also pride. I'm very proud of myself that I was a combatant. But there's a lot of shame, many thoughts afterwards, and for years now I'm still thinking about it.

PERSON IN
FATIGUES #2: Did I behave properly during that incident? Should I have opened fire? Did I not need to? Was it unnecessary?

PERSON IN
FATIGUES #3: I was a fighter, but for only one side, and... I don't know. I felt... a lot of hatred for them. A feeling of being exploited and... That they took everything out of you in impossible conditions, and then it sort of doesn't interest anybody.

    https://doi.org/10.11647/OBP.0223.33

PERSON IN

FATIGUES #4: I thought that I would be a combatant and defend... Sometimes, you do actually have the feeling that you're doing something but then when you think about it you realize it isn't exactly like that.

PERSON IN

FATIGUES #5: I remember being on the border and I would think to myself: seriously, they don't have the slightest idea what's happening a meter from their back, like, it's amazing. You step one meter away and you're in a completely different reality, and people don't know about it.

PERSON IN

FATIGUES #2: There's this reality, which is sometimes, you know, kind of surreal. Where an 18-year-old boy checks, and de-facto controls that day's fate of 200 people, adults, children, old women, not-so-old women.

The rhythm changes. Same rules.

PERSON IN

FATIGUES #4: And nobody knows this. People don't understand what's happening right next to them. And people who are there do things out of habit, it's their daily routine, it's what they do. And sometimes... it took me some time before what was really problematic about my service hit me. What's really problematic is that you don't understand what you're doing; because you're doing it as a fighter and not doing it as a thinking human being.

PERSON IN

FATIGUES #5: It's problematic that I, as a 19–20-year-old kid, control the lives of so many people, and that I have disproportionate authority. And honestly, I'll tell you the truth, I also have no idea what to do with it. I would check people without knowing why I'm doing it. And this whole situation where people are, every day, under military rule, and their day-to-day lives are determined by it. That's what's problematic. That's it, at large. That's what bothers me.

PERSON IN

FATIGUES #1: When I call someone over, just to call someone over, like, "come," because you know, you have to check, because you do have to check who the people are passing there in the street, yes, there are all sorts of incidents there, all sorts of stuff. So even when I called up someone to talk to them, just in order to prevent friction, because I see someone shitty approaching. Only to move the other one out of his way. And you see the man go: "yes, yes, what, what, no, I don't have anything, what." Like, in fear.

PERSON IN

FATIGUES #3: Seeing an old woman crawl to me on all fours just to say: "I know there's a curfew, that's why I'm not walking, but I have to go there, my kid is just here at the neighbour's, and I have to bring him home." And she comes back with a baby. She says to me: "Should I crawl on my knees?" I say to her: of course not, get up, go. A second later a soldier cocks his weapon at her just because she's passing by his post, and she gets back on her knees, so he won't... "I'm just getting my baby, I'm just..."

The rhythm changes. Same rules.

PERSON IN

FATIGUES #4: Like that. I say: why should she have to explain anything to me at all? She's walking in her neighbourhood. It's her neighbourhood, and she has to explain to me that she's just going to bring her baby. That's bad.

PERSON IN

FATIGUES #2: What shocked me, was that you would do things sitting behind a desk, in front of a computer, and you would cause colossal damage, collective and personal, to every single person there.

> As indicated in the footnote, the text in this scene has been taken from archival sources.
>
> From what you can glean in this text, what are the different real-world conflicts that the PERSONS IN FATIGUES might be referring to in this scene?

Trauma for life, psychological problems, killing, of course. Everything comes from the political echelon, which you've stopped believing in.

PERSON IN

FATIGUES #3: The first year was the hardest. Mostly because... I guess I thought more people would be thankful for what we are doing. That more people would appreciate that we are fighting. But... it can be isolating, this life.

The rhythm changes. Same rules.

The rhythm changes. Same rules.

The rhythm changes. Same rules.

GUIDE #1: How much longer is this going to go on?

GUIDE #2: As long as these folks want to keep playing the game!

GUIDE #1: How many of you want to move on?

A vote is taken. If more than half the audience wants to leave, they leave.

Otherwise, the rhythms keep changing and the seesawing continues.

Every so often the GUIDES take a vote. When more than half the audience votes to leave, the group leaves. They head to the next space, walking down a path that is composed of semi-wet clay.

Scene Twenty-One: The Disappeared & the Police

⊙ WATCH THE VIDEO

They enter a new room. There are different spaces within this one room:

- *A classroom*
- *FATHER #1 and CHILD #1's home*
- *FATHER #2 and CHILD #2's home*
- *A police station*

Two CHILDREN in a space that signifies a classroom. They sing the Urdu alphabet song.

CHILD #1 & #2: *Aliph mat a aam*

   Aliph a anaar

   Be ba billi

   Pe pa patang

   Te ta titili

   Te ta tamatar

   Se sa samar

   Jeem ja jahaaz

   Che cha chooha

   He ha hachaam

[The Urdu equivalent of "A for Apple;
B for Ball;
C for Cat;" etc.]

Aam: Mango
Anaar: Grapes
Billi: Cat
Patang: Kit
Titili: Butterfly
Tamatar: Tomato
Samar: Fruit
Jahaaz: Ship
Chooha: Mouse
Kharghosh: Rabbit

https://doi.org/10.11647/OBP.0223.34

Khe kha kharghosh

Da da darzi

Da da dol

Zaa za zakeera

At the end of the rhyme they walk to opposite ends of the room (their homes). They sit down and play quietly by themselves. Both fathers are already seated in the homes. FATHER #2 (of CHILD #2) is a policeman. Split scene.

FATHER #1: *Beta*, good you're home. What did you learn in school today?

CHILD #1: We learned the Urdu alphabet nursery rhyme, papa.

FATHER #2: The Urdu alphabet? But isn't that what you were learning two months ago? Are you still studying the same thing?

CHILD #2: School was closed for so many days last month n*a*, papa, so we are still learning the alphabet.

FATHER #1: At this rate, I don't know how you are going to study further and finish your exams.

CHILD #1: Don't worry, papa *ji*. I'll do well.

POLICEMEN enter the space with FATHER #1 and CHILD #1. When this is happening, FATHER #2 (CHIEF) goes to the police station space.

POLICEMEN: Hands up, in the name of the law!

CHILD #1: Daddy, Daddy, who are these people?

FATHER #1: Don't be afraid, my darlings!

POLICEMAN: Where is your wife, Uzma?

FATHER #1: I don't know!

CHILD #1: What do you mean, you don't know, Daddy! Mommy is in the bathroom! Mommy, Mommy. They're looking for you!

MOTHER: (*enters*) Who? What's happening?

POLICEMAN: This is what's happening! It's all over! Silence everyone! Everyone out. Let's go to the police station.

MOTHER: Not the child! They don't know anything about it!

POLICEMAN: Him too! Get out everyone.

They are all marched in a line to the police station.

FATHER #2
(CHIEF): Idiot! Why did you bring the kid?

POLICEMAN: You said everyone, Chief.

MOTHER: He is innocent.

FATHER #2
(CHIEF): I'll see if they're not already lost. Kid: who started the Kashmir issue?

MOTHER: Answer right, answer right!

CHILD #1: Jawaharlal Nehru!

FATHER #2
(CHIEF): When?

CHILD #1: 1947.

FATHER #2
(CHIEF): Where?

CHILD #1: At the UN. When Pakistani forces invaded Kashmir.

FATHER #2
(CHIEF): Exactly! Very good! (*Turns to FATHER #1*) Take him home. And don't be long.

POLICEMAN: Chief, what if he doesn't return?

FATHER #2
(CHIEF): She stays here. It's in her interest that he returns. (*Turns on FATHER #1*) Take my advice: be discreet. I'm doing you a favour. Don't be long.

FATHER #1: What are you going to do to her?

FATHER #2
(CHIEF): Nothing that I can tell you about.

MOTHER: Jehangir!

FATHER #1: Uzma, don't worry. I'll be back soon.

FATHER #2

(CHIEF): Take them home. Don't worry children, we don't have any small sacks in which to put your mother and throw her away.

MOTHER: Come, children! Give Mommy a kiss. Don't be afraid.

CHILD #1: The men seem nice, Mama!

FATHER #1 starts walking home with CHILD #1.

FATHER #1: Tell Grandma to pick up the medicines and cigarettes for me, OK?

CHILD #1: Yes, Papa.

FATHER #1: There's rice on the stove. Have it for dinner.

CHILD #1: If you're not there, I won't eat any rice! I won't eat any rice!

FATHER #1: Be good!

CHILD #1: Where are you going, Papa?

FATHER #1: I'm going to find Mama. You behave.

CHILD #1 watches FATHER #1 leave and begins to play quietly by himself.

FATHER #1 goes to the police station. During the goodbye scene between FATHER #1 and CHILD #1 the POLICEMEN put a sack on the MOTHER and take her out of the room.

FATHER #1: Here I am. Where's my wife?

FATHER #2

(CHIEF): Wife? What wife?

Silence. FATHER #1 stares at the CHIEF.

FATHER #1 walks back to his house. CHILD #1 and CHILD #2 move to the classroom.

CHILD #1 and CHILD #2 are back in the classroom and they continue with alphabet song. CHILD #1 keeps making the same mistake on one letter (any one). Every time he makes a mistake, they start the song from the beginning till CHILD #2 gets frustrated.

CHILD #1 & #2: *Aliph mat a aam*

   Aliph a anaar

   Be ba billi

   Pe pa patang

Te ta titili

Te ta tamatar

Se sa samar

Jeem ja jahaaz

Che cha chooha

Khe kha kharghosh

CHILD #2: What's wrong with you today? Why can't you remember this?

CHILD #1: I'm sorry...

CHILD #2: What's wrong?

CHILD #1: My mother hasn't been at home for a few days.

CHILD #2: Where has she gone?

CHILD #1: I don't know... These policemen came to our house. They seemed nice but after they took us to the station, I haven't seen my mother again.

CHILD #2: I'm sure the policemen had nothing to do with your mother not coming home.

CHILD #1: I'm sure you're right. But then, where is she?

CHILD #2: What does your father say?

CHILD #1: That my mother is at my grandmother's house.

CHILD #2: So, that's where she is, right?

CHILD #1: I don't believe him.

CHILD #2: Why not?

CHILD #1: He won't take me to my grandmother's house.

CHILD #2: Look. Let's try the alphabet song again. That'll take your mind off things.

They try the rhyme again. CHILD #1 makes the same mistake again. He begins to cry.

CHILD #2: Don't cry. Please. I'm sure your mother is fine. My mother has not been home in a long time either and I'm OK. You'll be fine too.

CHILD #1: Where is your mother?

CHILD #2: She is with my grandmother.

CHILD #1: Why?

CHILD #2: I don't know.

CHILD #1: Have you not seen her either?

CHILD #2: I see her every weekend. I go to my grandmother's house. See, maybe your father is just waiting for a weekend to take you to see her.

CHILD #1: Maybe.

CHILD #2: Do you want to study some more?

CHILD #1: I don't think so. I'm not able to focus today. Maybe we should just stop now.

CHILD #2: That's fine. I'll see you tomorrow?

CHILD #1: *Insh'Allah.*

> *Insh'Allah*
> If it is the will of God/ God willing

They go back to their homes. CHILD #1 enters his house and plays quietly; CHILD #2 walks in when:

FATHER #2
(CHIEF): What's wrong with you today? Why do you look so sad?

CHILD #2: Nothing, papa.

FATHER #2
(CHIEF): I can tell that something happened. What is it?

CHILD #2: One of my friends, papa *ji*. He says that his mother isn't at home anymore.

FATHER #2
(CHIEF): What happened to her? Is she sick?

CHILD #2: No, he said that one day she was there and then some men came — policemen — who took her away somewhere.

FATHER #2
(CHIEF): I see... Well, if they were policemen, I'm sure it was something they needed to ask her. Maybe his mother had some work or some relatives to visit after the policemen asked her their questions, and your friend doesn't know about that. Don't worry, I'm sure he's just missing his mother and she'll come back soon.

CHILD #2: Like my mom?

FATHER #2

(CHIEF): Hopefully his mother will come back sooner than your mother.

CHILD #2: Where has my mama gone papa?

FATHER #2

(CHIEF): You know that already. She has gone to stay with your grandparents for a little while.

CHILD #2: Why?

FATHER #2

(CHIEF): You know that grandmother is getting old and she needs some help taking care of grandfather.

CHILD #2: Is that all it is?

FATHER #2

(CHIEF): What else could it be?

Pause.

FATHER #2

(CHIEF): What is it, son?

CHILD #2: It's just that… Last time I visited mama, I heard her talking to my grandmother. I heard her say that she   finds it tough to live here with us. I heard her say that she is tired of people not treating her well because…

> What are the various layers of identity politics that Kashmiri police officers are mired in?

FATHER #2

(CHIEF): Because…?

CHILD #2: Because you're a police officer.

Silence. FATHER 2 exits angrily and goes to the police station. CHILD #2 sits on his own, dejected.

Focus goes to the other house. CHILD #1 is playing on his own when the same POLICEMEN as earlier enter again.

POLICEMAN: Where is your father?

CHILD #1: I don't know. Maybe he's outside?

Two other POLICEMEN have found the FATHER outside and drag him in.

POLICEMAN: Everyone out. Let's go to the police station.

They are all marched in a line to the police station.

FATHER #2
(CHIEF): Idiot! Why did you bring the kid again?

POLICEMAN: You said everyone, Chief.

FATHER #2
(CHIEF): You, child. Go home.

CHILD #1 hugs his father.

CHILD #1: Papa, these people are nice, right?

FATHER #1: Don't worry. Go home and make some tea. I'll be back soon.

CHILD #1 walks home while the POLICEMEN put a sack on the FATHER. Then they take him out of the room. After a little time has passed, where CHILD #1 plays with the rice his father has left him, CHILD #1 goes back to the police station.

CHILD #1: Sir. Where is my father?

FATHER #2
(CHIEF): Father? What father?

Silence. CHILD #1 stares at the CHIEF.

CHILD #1 and CHILD #2 move to the classroom. They are reciting the Urdu alphabet song again but this time, they are playing with cards that have pictures of the words next to each alphabet. When they reach the word Z, the picture of a policeman is shown.

CHILD #1 & #2: *Aliph mat a aam*

    Aliph a anaar

    Be ba billi

    Pe pa patang

    Te ta titili

    Te ta tamatar

    Se sa samar

    Jeem ja jahaaz

    Che cha chooha

Khe kha kharghosh

Zaa za - — .

CHILD #2 begins to tear up the card.

CHILD #1: What are you doing?

CHILD #2: Look at the picture.

CHILD #1: So? It's a policeman.

CHILD #2: My papa is a policeman. He is not a *zaalim*.

Silence.

> *Zaalim*
> Oppressor

CHILD #2: He is not. He is not. HE IS NOT.

CHILD #1: That's your opinion.

CHILD #2: No. He's not. He works so hard. He does so much for all of us. You cannot call him a *zaalim*.

Pause.

CHILD #1: My dad has gone too.

CHILD #2: What?

CHILD #1: My dad. The same men came back. Policemen. My dad is not there anymore.

CHILD #2: So? What are you implying?

CHILD #1: Are you stupid? Policemen came for my mother and then I don't see her again. They come from my father and then I don't see him again. What do you think happened?

CHILD #2: I think that policemen came because your parents must have done something wrong.

CHILD #1: My parents did NOTHING wrong.

CHILD #2: Then the policemen would not have done anything to them.

CHILD #1: You don't really believe that?

CHILD #2: Yes, I do. I believe that.

CHILD #1: Then you're really an idiot.

CHILD #1 and CHILD #2 get into a fight. Punches are thrown till both are too tired to fight. Their argument unresolved, the children both go back to their respective homes. They both sit in their homes, dazed.

Masked men come into the home of CHILD #1.

MASKED MAN: Where is your father?

CHILD #1: My father is not here.

MASKED MAN: Where is your mother?

CHILD #1: My mother isn't here either.

MASKED MAN: What are you doing here alone?

CHILD #1: Me? I'm not here. (*He starts repeating the line with growing intensity*) I am not here. I am not here. I am not here. I AM NOT HERE.

The MASKED MEN exchange glances, communicating their understanding that this boy has probably lost his mind. They leave. CHILD #1 remains there, rocking himself.

CHILD #2 is at home, cutting out the eyes from pictures of policemen in the newspaper. FATHER #2 walks in.

FATHER #2
(CHIEF): What's this nonsense?

CHILD #2: Papa, why do people hate you?

Pause.

FATHER #2
(CHIEF): Make me some tea.

CHILD #2: When will mamma come home?

Pause.

FATHER #2
(CHIEF): Make me some tea.

CHILD #2: Papa —

FATHER #2
(CHIEF): Make me some tea.

CHILD #2 goes to make tea. FATHER #2 (CHIEF) looks at his policeman's hat. His expressions flicker. Change. He throws the hat on the ground. Picks it back up. Exits.

CHILD #2 enters with the tea. Noticing that his father has left, CHILD #2 picks up the scissors. He begins to angle them toward his eyes. Just as it gets uncomfortable, when CHILD #2's intentions to hurt himself become apparent —

GUIDE #1: Son —

CHILD #2 drops the tea and runs out of the room.

The spilling of the chai brings CHILD #1 one out of his reverie. He begins to sing.

While he sings, he picks up stone souvenirs and hands one to each audience member. The stone is covered with a story. Something like An Unstoppable Storm *(Geelani, 2017).*

As CHILD #1 finishes handing out souvenirs, the GUIDES take the audience down the next path, which is composed with extracts about Kashmir from school textbooks around the world. CHILD #1's song can be heard on the walk.

Scene Twenty-Two: The Hope

 WATCH THE VIDEO

The audience walks into a room that has actors who are wearing masks. Masks on the backs of their heads. A poem from the Zapatistas (Enlace Zapatista, 2013).

ACTOR #1: Our strength, if we have one, is in this recognition:

we are who we are,

and there are others who are who they are,

and others who we still don't have the words to name,

and are nevertheless who they are.

When we say "we" we are not absorbing and, in doing so, subordinating identities,

but rather emphasizing the bridges that exist between different sufferings and different rebellions.

We are equal because we are different.

ACTOR #2: We have learned from our dead that

diversity and difference are not a weakness,

but rather a strength from which to birth, from the ashes of the old,

the new world that we want,

that we need,

that we deserve.

ACTOR #3: They believe that they are the only ones; we know that we are just one of many.

> Look into some of the active rebel groups in Kashmir.
>
> Do you see any similarities between one or more of these groups, and the Zapatistas in Mexico?
>
> What are some of the marked differences between the Zapatistas' struggles and what is happening in Kashmir?

https://doi.org/10.11647/OBP.0223.35

They look for ways to make themselves comfortable; we look for ways to serve.

They look for ways to lead; we look for ways to accompany.

They look at how much you earn; we at how much is lost.

They look for what is; we, for what could be.

ACTOR #4: They see numbers; we see people.

They calculate statistics; we, histories.

They speak; we listen.

They look at how they look; we look at the gaze.

They look to see how you can take advantage of the current conjuncture; we look to see how we can create it.

They concern themselves with the broken windows; we concern ourselves with the rage that broke them.

When conducting interview-based research, especially as an outsider, one is often confronted with the notion of truth. How do we know when we are being told the truth? How do we know if we are being lied to?

Don't we owe it to our interviewees to assume that they are telling us the truth?

And yet, don't we owe it to ourselves to be cautious? To ensure that we are not being gullible?

What are some practical strategies, if any, that an interviewer might use as a litmus test?

ACTOR #5: They look at the many; we at the few.

They see impassable walls; we see the cracks.

They look at possibilities; we look at what was impossible until the eve of its possibility.

They search for mirrors; we for windows.

Them and us are not the same.

Our strength, if we have one, is in this recognition:

we are who we are.

And who are "they"?

ACTORS exit.

Silence.

GUIDE #1: Tell me. As an outsider coming in to learn about Kashmir, what kind of stories were you looking for?

GUIDE #2: I wasn't looking for any one type of story in particular. I knew I didn't want to be a 'dark tourist' you know? And only ask people for the stories of their pain. So usually, I let them direct the conversation and share what they wanted to share.

GUIDE #1: What if you were lied to?

GUIDE #2: Then I was lied to.

GUIDE #1: Did you come up with a way to evaluate which stories were true and which stories were not?

GUIDE #2: Is there any fool-proof way to evaluate such a thing? I accepted every story that was shared with me to be a truth, in one way or the other.

GUIDE #1: But isn't accepting everyone's story as being true — pardon my use of the term — naïve?

GUIDE #2: Naïve? But wouldn't it be more misguided to approach everyone as if they were lying?

GUIDE #1: We're not going to agree on this, are we?

GUIDE #2: You know, let's play a game with these folks here and see how easy it is to spot a lie. OK? As an experiment.

Ladies and gentlemen: this game is called "Two truths and a lie." One of you starts by telling us three things about yourself: two of those statements must be true; one must be a lie. Based on what we've come to know of you in the last day, I'm going to ask my friend here (*pointing to GUIDE #1*) to identify which statement is the lie. One person at a time. OK?

Any questions are answered. GUIDE #2 shows an example, if needed.

The audience plays the game. GUIDE #1 tries to ascertain the lie in the audience members' statements. Once all audience members who are willing have participated:

GUIDE #2: Not so easy, no?

GUIDE #1: Not too difficult, either.

GUIDE #2: You just won't let me have the last word, will you?!

GUIDE #1: Shall we move on?

They smile at each other. They move on to the next space, down a path installed with masks.

Imagine this.

You've just conducted an interview with someone about an aspect of income inequality in your community.

You know that this person is either lying explicitly, misrepresenting the truth, or lying by omission.

Now, ethically, you cannot put words into this interviewee's mouth when you use their words in a piece of Documentary Theatre.
So, what can you do?

What are some aesthetic strategies that you could use to problematize the interviewee's contributions, without altering their actual words?

The Last Coalition

Like the ones that came before it, this COALITION is a space of collaborative creation; of a group of people coming together, albeit temporarily, to "make something": an atmosphere, a spirit, a hope, a recognition.

Audience members return to the same space that they entered at the very beginning of their time in Chronicles from Kashmir: *you remember, the tourism office? This time, however, amidst the brochures and all the other tourist paraphernalia, there are actors frozen in various positions. Each of the actors represents a scene that was showcased over the course of the 24-hour experience.*

It is suggested that the following characters and actions/lines are represented. If the same performer played more than one of the characters below during the original scene, different actors can play those characters. The point at which actors unfreeze for their actions/lines can be found later in this scene.

Scene	Character	Action/ Line
The Experiment	THE TEACHER	"I will not press the button"
The Migration	THE DOCTOR	"Am I not free?" *said from inside the trunk that he crawled into during the scene*
The Man & Woman	THE WOMAN	"Because I am a woman. And this, is a war."
The Artists	THE ART CRITIC/ FELLOW ARTIST/ CULTURAL AGENT	"It needs to be something we can sell. Nothing too realistic. Nothing too experimental. Nothing too this. Nothing too that. It has to be just right."

  https://doi.org/10.11647/OBP.0223.36

Scene	Character	Action/ Line
The Puppets	A PUPPET	*The puppets' strings have been visibly cut. S/he moves wildly, erratically. Repeats.* "Now what?"
The Incarcerated	A PRISONER	*Repeats the following words in no particular order.* "Terrorist, Rebel, Militant, Martyr, Freedom Fighter, Revolutionary, Soldier."
The Soldiers	A SOLDIER	*Holds the gun to his head. Points it at someone in the audience. Holds it to his head. Points it at a fellow actor. And so on and so forth.*
The Argumentation Cultures	A character who is a mix of the MOTHER, FATHER and TEACHER	"Don't raise your voice when you are talking to people. Disagreements are a waste of time. If you meet someone who doesn't agree with you, just walk away. You need to tell people what you think. Be direct. Confront a problem head on. Sometimes you need to use your fists. It's best not to fight. People never change their minds. Make sure you are heard. Make sure your voice is heard. A hug solves everything. Just agree to disagree, no? Don't you dare argue with someone older than you. Don't argue with your husband. Stand your ground. Fight for what you believe in. It's always important to be polite. Act your age. You need to learn how to argue politely."
The Sikhs	THE DIRECTOR	*Arranges a row of turbans as a memorial.*
The Apples	ACTOR #2	*Pulls out apples from a sack and throws them to different audience members; all while saying:* "Use the apple to express yourself."
The Water	A CHILD	"Anyone want to go to the water with me?!"
The Village City Love Affair	THE WIFE	"I've had enough of your brother telling me what us city people are like."

Scene	Character	Action/ Line
The Mirrors and a Poetic Lament	AN ACTOR	"They say I should write hope They say I should write difference They say I should write paths And options And ways And roads And bridges But sometimes, This is all there is to write."
The Pelters	A PELTER	*Plays with a stone in his hands while saying:* "It depends on who you ask."
The Banalities	A SOLDIER	"We wait. For the other shoe to drop. For the next stone to be thrown. And finally, there is something for us to do."
The Time	AN ACTOR	*Sings the song about time that is sung by the GUIDE during the scene.*
The Women	AN ACTOR	"Either you will succumb or rise. I chose to rise. I collected my scattered parts to rise. Nobody fights for us. Nobody fought for me. You have to fight your own battle Yes, I am a feminist."

Scene	Character	Action/ Line
The Game Show	THE HOST	"What is the most feasible solution to Kashmir's conflicts? Create more ways for Kashmiris to identify with India Search for a political solution that involves discussions with Kashmir, India, and Pakistan Increase tourism to Kashmir None of the above"
The Hideout	A KASHMIRI	"You are going to leave. I'm the one who has to stay here. I'm the one who has to live with the consequences of this..."
The Return	A PANDIT & MUSLIM in the same body	"Find a way out?"
The Disappeared and the Police	THE KASHMIRI POLICEMAN	*He stands silently. Playing with his cap.*
The Hope	A MASKED FIGURE	"They concern themselves with the broken windows, we concern ourselves with the rage that broke it. Them and us are not the same."

Would your choices for the highlighted character, action, and/ or line in each scene stay the same as, or differ from, what has been suggested in the table above?

If you could redo the recap section entirely, with the only restriction being that you have to somehow remind audiences of material that they encountered in the previous 24 hours, what would your approach look like?

When the audience enters this space, the GUIDES ignore the actors — who remain silent and frozen in position, until described otherwise, later in this scene. The GUIDES walk over to the middle of the room, where there are different kinds of props/costumes/materials that are placed there. The audience is asked to form a circle with the GUIDES.

GUIDE #1: You know, we have been showing you our experiences from Kashmir over the last day and... now, before we part ways, we want you to do something for us. So, we ask that you — individually, in pairs, in groups, however you wish — share something in response to what you have witnessed here. You can share your response as a song, as a drawing, as a story, as a dance, as silence... whatever you want. We just want some of your responses to what you have witnessed over the last 24 hours. Could you all decide how you want to do this? Alone or in groups or...?

The GUIDES stand back and let the audience figure it out. Once groups have been formed:

GUIDE #2: How much time would you like to prepare — before presenting your different responses to the group?

The GUIDES stand back and let the audience figure it out. Once they have decided a time, the GUIDES only function is to keep reminding the spectators how much time they have left: a drumbeat is used to precede an announcement of how much time is remaining.

Refreshments are served while the spectators use the agreed upon duration to "make" a response.

Once the drum has sounded to indicate that the time for preparation is over, the GUIDES facilitate each person/pair/group's presentation of their work. When a spectator(s) presents, there is a spotlight that is shown on them: what they're sharing is special; it's something that should be paid attention. This spotlight turns off as soon as each individual/pair/group indicates the end of their presentation, and the room reverts to "normal" lighting until the next each individual/pair/group volunteer to present. There is no discussion following any each individual/pair/group's presentation. The presentations follow each other, with the changes in lighting and a drumbeat from the GUIDES to indicate the beginning of a new presentation.

Once all the audience members have shared their work, the drumbeats three times. A spotlight — the same one that was used for the spectators' presentations — shines on one actor. They perform their action/line — described in the table at the start of this scene — and repeat the stated action/line until the GUIDES give them a drumbeat as their signal to freeze. The spotlight moves in sync with the drumbeat, to another performer. That next actor performs their line/action. So on and so forth. Consider this a "flashback," if you will: of many of the voices that audience members have experienced through their time in Chronicles from Kashmir.

Once the last actor has finished their action/line, the drumbeats abound. The actors unfreeze and move through the audience in varied ways — weaving in and out of their midst, sometimes making eye contact, sometimes shaking a hand — before purposefully exiting the room. Once all the actors have exited the space, the drumbeats stop.

GUIDE #1: As I told you when we began our time together yesterday, we believe it is important to consider how outsiders see and understand our home: so that we can better understand the outsider's place in Kashmir's future, if there is a place at all...

The term "outsider" is one that we've used a lot in this experience and as we get ready to part ways, I want to leave you with a question: Who, really, is an outsider in Kashmir? Is an outsider only the person like my friend here (*pointing to GUIDE #2*) who was not born or brought up in Kashmir? Or can an outsider also be found in those Kashmiris who do not conform to what others want or expect from them? Can an outsider be found in the Kashmiri who, in colluding with outsiders, becomes one? Or is there, in some way, an outsider inside every Kashmiri?

The GUIDES smile at each other and prepare to exit. As they exit, they shake each audience member's hand and give them one last stone souvenir. This last stone has wrapped around it any contact information that the production company would like to leave the spectators with. Or perhaps, an article like Chris Jenkins' (2012) Belfast's immoral "conflict tourism."

Once the GUIDES exit, the crew members on "audience duty" ask audience members to return any props/costumes they might have used for their presentations, to gather their bags with the stone souvenirs, and to follow the crew members to the bus. The belongings that the spectators arrived with should have previously been loaded on the bus.

When the audience members head to the bus, they walk down a path that is composed of doors and windows.

The same ACTOR who checked the audience's IDs and bags the previous day boards the bus with them. They are dropped off where they met 24 hours earlier.

> Given the pedagogical objectives of *Chronicles from Kashmir*, what kinds of post-performance mechanisms (if any) should be put in place in order to sustain the longer-term engagement of spectators?
>
> Who might be the ideal target audience for this annotated, multimedia resource of *Chronicles from Kashmir*?

Bibliography

Ahmad, A. 2015. *Bad Muslim*. CounterPunch.org. https://www.counterpunch.org/2015/01/12/bad-muslim/print/

Ahmed, M. 2016. *Mediah Visits the Inclusive Mosque*. Sisterhood. http://sister-hood.com/mediah-ahmed/mediah-visits-inclusive-mosque/

Ali, A.S. 2003. *Call Me Ishmael Tonight: A Book of Ghazals*. W. W. Norton and Company Inc.

Amnesty International. 2015. *Denied: Failures in Accountability For Human Rights Violations By Security Force Personnel in Jammu and Kashmir*. https://www.amnesty.org/en/documents/asa20/1874/2015/en/

Bashir, S. 2015. *A Bunker in Every Mind*. Himal Southasian. http://himalmag.com/bunker-every-mind-kashmir-memoir/

BBC. 2012. *Indian Army Suicides Blamed on 'Poor Leadership'*. http://www.bbc.com/news/world-asia-india-17936070

Bharucha, R. 2003. *Theatre and the World: Performance and the Politics of Culture*. London: Routledge. https://doi.org/10.4324/9780203168172 ,

Bhutto, Z.A. 2017. *Mussalmaan Musclemen: Dissecting Masculinity In Pakistan Through Art*. Huffington Post. https://www.huffingtonpost.com/entry/mussalmaan-musclemen-dissecting-masculinity-in-pakistan_us_5935be64e4b033940169cd09?ncid=tweetlnkush pmg00000054

Bosoer, F. & Finchelstein, F. 2014. *Argentina's Truth Commission at 30*. Al Jazeera. http://america.aljazeera.com/opinions/2014/1/argentina-conadeptruthcommissionhumanrights.html

Chowdhury, K.L. 2016. *Kashmiri Pandits remember January 19, 1990: 'It is for your own good to leave'*. Scroll.in. https://scroll.in/article/802093/kashmiri-pandits-remember-january-19-1990-it-is-for-your-own-good-to-leave

Chronicles from Kashmir. 2017. https://youtu.be/izeXhNK-_HQ

Ded, Lal. n.d. *To Learn the Scriptures is Easy*. Poemhunter. https://www.poemhunter.com/poem/to-learn-the-scriptures-is-easy/

Dinesh, N. 2013. *Theatre & War: Notes from the Field*. Cambridge: Open Book Publishers. https://doi.org/10.11647/obp.0099

El Saadawi, N. 2017. *Capitalism and Fundamentalism Are Interdependent*. Sisterhood. http://sister-hood.com/nawal-el-saadawi/capitalism-religious-fundamentalism-interdependent/

Enlace Zapatista. 2013. *Them and Us. VI. – The Gaze*. http://enlacezapatista.ezln.org.mx/2013/02/09/them-and-us-vi-the-gaze/

Ensemble Kashmir Theatre Akademi (EKTA). 2018. www.ektakashmir.org.in

Gambaro, G. 1992. *Information for Foreigners: Three Plays by Griselda Gambaro.* Evanston, Illinois: Northwestern University Press.

Geelani, G. 2017. *Cop's Conscience.* Kashmir Ink. http://www.kashmirink.in/news/reportage/cop-s-conscience/440.html

Geelani, G. 2017. *POETS AND REBELS.* Kashmir Ink. http://www.kashmirink.in/news/coverstory/poets-and-rebels/361.html

Grammarly. 2014. *How To Write Your Manifesto In 5 Steps.* Huffington Post. https://www.huffingtonpost.com/grammarly/write-manifesto_b_5575496.html

Haedicke, S.C. 2002. The Politics of Participation: Un Voyage Pas Comme Les Autres Sur Les Chemins De'L Exil. *Theatre Topics.* 12(2): 99-118. https://doi.org/10.1353/tt.2002.0011

Hafizi, M. 2015. *Leaving Home.* Himal Southasian. http://himalmag.com/leaving-home-short-story/

Harris, D. n.d. *Weddings in a War Zone.* ABC News. http://abcnews.go.com/WNT/International/story?id=2808751

Hashim, A. 2011. *Kashmir in the Collective Imagination.* Al Jazeera. http://www.aljazeera.com/indepth/spotlight/kashmirtheforgottenconflict/2011/08/201186121738346838.html

Henley, J. 2016. *Anders Breivik's Human Rights Violated in Prison, Norway Court Rules.* The Guardian. https://www.theguardian.com/world/2016/apr/20/anders-behring-breiviks-human-rights-violated-in-prison-norway-court-rules

Hindustan Times. 2017. *310 Army Personnel Committed Suicide Since 2014: Government.* https://www.hindustantimes.com/india-news/310-army-personnel-committed-suicide-since-2014-government/story-68XnhGfM2RAlGvZS4bcwjL.html

Hiremath, A. 2013. *The Gastronomical Affair of a Kashmiri Pandit Wedding.* The Alternative. http://www.thealternative.in/lifestyle/the-gastronomical-affair-of-a-kashmiri-pandit-wedding/

International People's Tribunal on Human Rights and Justice in Kashmir (IPTK). 2009. *Buried Evidence: Unknown, Unmarked, and Mass Graves in Indian-administered Kashmir.* http://www.kashmirprocess.org/reports/graves/toc.html

International Peoples' Tribunal on Human Rights and Justice in Indian-Administered Kashmir [IPTK] and The Association of Parents of Disappeared Persons [APDP]. 2015. *Structures of Violence: The Indian State in Jammu and Kashmir.* https://jkccs.files.wordpress.com/2017/05/structures-of-violence-e28093-main-report.pdf

Jenkins, C. 2012. *Belfast's Immoral 'Conflict Tourism'.* The Guardian. https://www.theguardian.com/commentisfree/2012/may/07/belfast-immoral-conflict-tourism

Kak, S. 2011. *Unity My Freedom Has Come.* Penguin India.

Kakar, H. 2017. *Suicides and Fratricide: Indian Army Takes Care of Its Soldiers, Stop Maligning It.* https://www.dailyo.in/voices/indian-army-suicides-pressure-counter-insurgency-us-military/story/1/20114.html

Kaul, N. 2013. *The Idea of India and Kashmir.* Daily O. http://www.india-seminar.com/2013/643/643_nitasha_kaul.htm

Kaul, S. 2015. *Of Gardens and Graves: Essays on Kashmir | Poems in Translation.* Three Essays Collective.

Lewis, R. 2014. *How Different Cultures Understand Time.* Business Insider. http://www.businessinsider.com/how-different-cultures-understand-time-2014-5

Liu, M. 2016. Verbal Communication Styles and Culture. *Oxford Research Encyclopedia of Communication*. https://www.doi.org/10.1093/acrefore/9780190228613.013.162

Madan, T.N. 2015. *Old Memories and Recent Encounters from a Kashmir We Have Irretrievably Lost*. The Wire.in. https://thewire.in/17639/old-memories-and-recent-encounters-from-a-world-we-have-irretrievably-lost/

Maqbool, M. 2016. *Here's How Kashmiri Cartoonists Are Playing with Their Pain*. The Wire.in. https://thewire.in/59507/kashmiri-cartoonists-draw-their-tragedy/

Maqbool, M. 2017. *Why Are the Armed Forces in Kashmir Plagued by so Many Suicides and Fratricides?* The Wire.in https://thewire.in/182639/kashmir-armed-forces-suicides-fratricides/

Manecksha, F. 2014. *Autonomy under Siege*. Himal Southasian. http://himalmag.com/autonomy-siege/

MaryScullyReports.2016.*TributeToTheStone-ThrowersOfPalestinian&KashmiriIntifada*.http://www.maryscullyreports.com/tribute-to-the-stone-throwers-of-palestinian-kashmiri-intifada/

McLeod, S. 2007. *The Milgram Experiment*. Simply Psychology. https://www.simplypsychology.org/milgram.html

McNaughton, C. & Bukhari, F. 2017. *Kashmir's Stone-Pelters Face Off Against Pellet Guns*. Reuters. https://widerimage.reuters.com/story/kashmirs-stone-pelters-face-off-against-pellet-guns

Murthy, R.S. & Lakshminarayana, R. 2006. *Mental Health Consequences of War: A Brief Review of Research Findings*. National Centre for Biotechnology Information. https://www.ncbi.nlm.nih.gov/pmc/articles/PMC1472271/

Muzafar, I. 2017. *Five Poems by Insha Muzafar*. Wande Magazine. http://www.wandemag.com/five-poems-by-insha/

Ohlheiser, A. 2013. *Malcolm Gladwell's Cockpit Culture Theory and the Asiana Crash*. The Atlantic. https://www.theatlantic.com/national/archive/2013/07/malcolm-gladwells-cockpit-culture-theory-everywhere-after-asiana-crash/313442/

Pandit, L. 1996. *Anantnag*. http://www.koausa.org/Books/Sukeshi/poem6.html

Pandit, R. 2017. *Over 100 Military Personnel Commit Suicide Every Year*. Times of India. https://timesofindia.indiatimes.com/india/over-100-military-personnel-commit-suicide-every-year/articleshow/57579464.cms

Pandita, R. 2013. *On Kashmir and its Stories*. Forbes India. http://www.forbesindia.com/article/recliner/rahulpanditaonkashmiranditsstories/34787/1

Pandita, R. 2016. *The Ugly Truth Behind a 'Heartwarming' Story of Muslims Performing a Kashmiri Pandit's Last Rites*. Scroll.in. https://scroll.in/article/803087/the-ugly-truth-behind-a-heartwarming-story-of-muslims-performing-a-kashmiri-pandits-last-rites

Ramachandran, S. 2013. *India's Troubled Soldiers: A String of Violent Incidents Reveals Some Festering Problems in India's Military*. The Diplomat. https://thediplomat.com/2013/12/indias-troubled-soldiers/

Rana, T & Berry, M. 2015. *A Woman Did That? Thoughts on Women Perpetrators of Violence*. Political Violence at a Glance. http://politicalviolenceataglance.org/2015/12/17/a-woman-did-that-thoughts-on-women-perpetrators-of-violence/

Rath, B. 2017. *Why We Need to Talk About the Condition of India's Prisons*. The Wire.in. https://thewire.in/161064/india-prison-conditions/

Saatchi Art. 2018. *Masood Hussain*. https://www.saatchiart.com/account/artworks/426094

Sajad, M. 2015. *Munnu: A Boy from Kashmir*. London: Fourth Estate.

Scroll.in. 2016. *A Query for Rahul Pandita: Why Are You Ignoring the Existence of a Kashmiri Brotherhood? A Selection of Readers' Opinions on the Piece Debunking a Story of Solidarity Involving a Kashmiri Pandit's Last Rites.* https://scroll.in/article/803309/a-query-for-rahul-pandita-why-are-you-ignoring-the-existence-of-a-kashmiri-brotherhood

Scroll.in. 2017. *Readers' Comments: 'Kashmir belongs equally to Pandits who were driven out, Harsh Mander'.* https://scroll.in/article/840154/readers-comments-harsh-mander-kashmir-equally-belongs-to-pandits-who-were-driven-out

Shabir, M. 2017. *Friday Notes on Kashmir: 23 June 2017.* Wande Magazine. http://www.wandemag.com/friday-notes-on-kashmir/

Shameem, B. 2016. *Kashmir's Exile Poetry: An Aesthetic of Loss.* Countercurrents. https://countercurrents.org/2016/06/19/kashmirs-exile-poetry-an-aesthetic-of-loss/

Sharma, V. 2016. *A Pandit POV: Why the Discussion on Jammu and Kashmir Is Half-Baked and Dishonest.* Scroll.in. https://scroll.in/article/813509/why-the-discourse-on-jammu-and-kashmir-is-dishonest-and-half-baked

Sharma, V. 2017. *The Prolonged Wait: Kashmir Lives on in the Hearts and Minds of Pandits.* Scroll.in. https://scroll.in/article/834017/the-prolonged-wait-kashmir-lives-on-in-the-hearts-and-minds-of-pandits

Sirsa, M.S. 2017. *Sharing the Pain of Sikhs in Kashmir.* https://mssirsa.com/2017/09/11/raising-the-issue-of-minority-sikhs-in-kashmir-with-cm-mehbooba-mufti/

Tamim, B. 2016. *Kashmir's Mental Health Crisis.* Al Jazeera. http://www.aljazeera.com/indepth/features/2016/06/kashmir-mental-health-crisis-160620085520339.html

Tihar Jail Initiative. 2010. http://tihartj.nic.in/bakery_biscuits.asp

Times of India. 2015. *Most of the Jails in Jammu and Kashmir Overcrowded.* https://timesofindia.indiatimes.com/city/srinagar/Most-of-the-jails-in-Jammu-and-Kashmir-overcrowded/articleshow/49236777.cms

Vasudeva, S. 2017. *Beyond Wazwan: A Peek into the Cuisine of Kashmiri Pandits.* NDTV. https://food.ndtv.com/opinions/beyond-wazwan-a-peek-into-the-cuisine-of-kashmiri-pandits-1275847

Wani, W.M. 2013. *Art of Protest in Kashmir.* Kashmir Lit. http://www.kashmirlit.org/art-of-protest-and-agony-in-kashmir/

Zia, A. 2008. *Q & A with Sanjay Kak.* Kashmir Lit. http://www.kashmirlit.org/q-a-with-sanjay-kak-2/

Zinn, H. 2004. *Artists in Times of War.* https://zinnedproject.org/materials/artists-in-times-of-war/

About the Team

Alessandra Tosi was the managing editor for this book.

Lucy Barnes performed the copy-editing and proofreading.

Anna Gatti designed the cover using InDesign. The cover was produced in InDesign using Fontin (titles) and Calibri (text body) fonts.

Luca Baffa typeset the book in InDesign. The text font is Tex Gyre Pagella; the heading font is Noto Sans. Luca created all of the editions — paperback, hardback, EPUB, MOBI, PDF, HTML, and XML — the conversion is performed with open source software freely available on our GitHub page (https://github.com/OpenBookPublishers).

This book need not end here...

Share

All our books — including the one you have just read — are free to access online so that students, researchers and members of the public who can't afford a printed edition will have access to the same ideas. This title will be accessed online by hundreds of readers each month across the globe: why not share the link so that someone you know is one of them?

This book and additional content is available at:

https://doi.org/10.11647/OBP.0223

Customise

Personalise your copy of this book or design new books using OBP and third-party material. Take chapters or whole books from our published list and make a special edition, a new anthology or an illuminating coursepack. Each customised edition will be produced as a paperback and a downloadable PDF.

Find out more at:

https://www.openbookpublishers.com/section/59/1

Like Open Book Publishers

Follow @OpenBookPublish

Read more at the Open Book Publishers BLOG

Applied Theatre Praxis Series

About the series

Applied Theatre Praxis (ATP) is an OBP series that focuses on Applied Theatre practitioner-researchers who use their rehearsal rooms as "labs"; spaces in which theories are generated, explored and/or experimented with before being implemented in contentious and/or vulnerable contexts. ATP invites writing that draws from the author/s' praxis to generate theory for diverse manifestations of Applied Theatre.

The series is overseen by an international board of experts and its books subjected to rigorous peer review. ATP invites writing that is focussed on "theory building" , writing that draws from the author's praxis to generate theory for diverse manifestations of Applied Theatre.

Given OBPs flexible publishing format, this series welcomes both traditional-length and short-form monographs. Furthermore, since OBP's approach allows for the integration of multimedia, books in the ATP Series could contain audio-visual documentation that explicitly showcases the dynamism that is involved in theatrical research.

Editorial Board

You can find more information about this series at

https://www.openbookpublishers.com/section/81/1

OpenBook Publishers

www.ingramcontent.com/pod-product-compliance
Lightning Source LLC
Chambersburg PA
CBHW041427270326
41932CB00027B/3411